MUMBAI
26/11
A DAY OF INFAMY

MUMBAI
26/11
A DAY OF INFAMY

B RAMAN

Lancer • New Delhi • Frankfort, IL
www.lancerpublishers.com

LANCER

Published in the United States by

The Lancer International Inc
19558 S. Harlem Ave., Suite 1,
Frankfort, IL. 60423.

First published in India by

Lancer Publishers & Distributors
2/42 (B) Sarvapriya Vihar,
New Delhi-110016

Printed and bound in India.

ISBN-13: 978-1-935501-16-9 • ISBN-10: 1-935501-16-X

Online Military Bookshop
www.lancerpublishers.com
_____
IDR Net Edition
www.indiandefencereview.com

CONTENTS

PREFACE

Even while holding talks with the US on peace in the Pacific, the Japanese Empire secretly and treacherously planned and carried out massive surprise attacks from the air and the sea on Pearl Harbor in Hawaii on December 7, 1941, killing a large number of American military personnel and civilians and destroying the US naval base there.

In an address to the US Congress the next day, which came to be known as the "Day of Infamy" speech, the then US President Franklin D. Roosevelt said: "Yesterday, December 7, 1941 — a date which will live in infamy — the United States of America was suddenly and deliberately attacked by naval and air forces of the Empire of Japan. The United States was at peace with that Nation and, at the solicitation of Japan, was still in conversation with its Government and its Emperor looking towards the maintenance of peace in the Pacific. Indeed, one hour after Japanese air squadrons had commenced bombing in Oahu, the Japanese Ambassador to the United States and his colleague delivered to the Secretary of State their reply to a recent American message. While this reply stated that it seemed useless to continue the existing diplomatic negotiations, it contained no threat or hint of war or armed attack. It will be recorded that the distance of Hawaii from Japan makes it obvious that the attack was deliberately planned many days or even weeks ago. During the intervening time the Japanese Government had deliberately sought to deceive the United States by false statements and expressions of hope for continued peace … The facts of yesterday speak for themselves. The people of the United States have already formed their opinions and well understand the implications to the very life and safety of our Nation. As Commander-in-Chief of the Army and Navy I have directed that all measures be taken for our defense. Always will we remember the character of the onslaught against us. No matter how long it may take us to overcome this premeditated invasion, the American people in their righteous might will win through to absolute victory. I believe I interpret the will of the Congress and of the people when I assert that we will not only defend ourselves to the uttermost but will make very certain that this form of treachery shall never endanger us again. Hostilities exist. There is no blinking at the fact that our people, our territory, and our interests are in grave danger. With confidence in our armed forces — with the unbounded determination of our people — we will gain the inevitable triumph — so help us God. I ask that the Congress declare that since the unprovoked and dastardly attack by Japan on Sunday, December seventh, a state of war has existed between the United States and the Japanese Empire."

Sixty-seven years later, the world saw another day of infamy on November 26, 2008. Around 8-30 PM, a group of 10 Pakistani terrorists belonging to the Lashkar-e-Toiba (LeT), an ally of Al Qaeda and a strategic asset of Pakistan's Inter-Services Intelligence (ISI), secretly landed in the seafront area of Mumbai, the jewel of

India and the business and financial capital of a newly-emerging economic power, divided themselves into four groups and went around spreading death and destruction over a wide area in the seafront.

It was a commando-style raid by a group of specially trained jihadis, the like of which the world had not seen before.

One group killed the ordinary people of the city — innocent men, women and children. Many in a railway station. Some in a hospital. And some others on the roads and elsewhere.

Two others, after killing the diners and staff of a restaurant, entered and occupied two five-star hotels frequented by the business and social elite of India and the world. They remained in occupation of the hotels for nearly 60 hours and engaged in a confrontation with the security forces before they were killed.

The fourth group forced its way into a Jewish cultural-cum-religious centre, took its six inmates — four Israelis and two with dual US nationality — hostages, tortured them and finally killed them before the security forces could intervene. Among those tortured and killed by them was an Israeli woman, who was expecting a baby.

It was one of the most treacherous attacks in the history of terrorism. And one of the most dastardly.

As treacherous and as dastardly as Al Qaeda's attacks in the US homeland on 9/11.

But Al Qaeda was not the tool of any State. No State was using it to attack the US.

The LeT was. It was the tool of Pakistan's military-intelligence establishment.

It has been since its creation in the 1980s during the so-called jihad against the Soviet troops in Afghanistan.

The ISI used it in Afghanistan in the 1980s.

It has been using it against India since 1993.

Initially in Jammu & Kashmir. Subsequently, in other parts of India.

The LeT helped the ISI in its strategic agenda against India.

This did not stop it from helping Al Qaeda in its operations against the West.

The fact that post-9/11, the LeT had started acting as the strategic ally of Al Qaeda did not come in the way of its continued role as the strategic asset of the ISI.

This was not the first act of mass casualty terrorism carried out by the LeT in Mumbai.

This was the second.

The first was in July 2006 when terrorists trained by it carried out a series of explosions in the suburban trains of Mumbai, killing over 170 innocent civilians.

Instead of reacting with as much righteous indignation and force against Pakistan as Roosevelt did against the Japanese Empire for its act of treachery, we chose to give it the benefit of doubt.

Within two months of this act of treachery, we entered into an agreement with Pakistan for setting up a joint counter-terrorism mechanism as if Pakistan looked upon the LeT as a terrorist organization.

It never did.

We entered into peace talks with Pakistan. Through governmental and non-governmental channels. Composite dialogue, it was called.

Even as these talks were going on, the ISI was preparing two other groups of terrorists for use against India.

One group attacked the Indian Embassy in Kabul in the first week of July, 2008.

What brave statements we made after the Kabul attack! We threatened to have the ISI destroyed!

The Pakistanis and the ISI must have chuckled within themselves.

Imagine the Government of India translating its brave words into action!

It has never done it.

The Pakistanis must have been certain that it will never do it in the future.

So as the peace talks were going on and as the so-called joint counter-terrorism mechanism was holding one meeting after another, a new group of terrorists was being trained commando style.

Initially, they were trained in camps in Pakistan-occupied Kashmir.

Subsequently, in Karachi.

Then, they sailed to Mumbai and attacked under the darkness of the early night.

The Japanese Pearl Harbor attack lasted just a few hours.

The LeT attack lasted 60 hours plus.

The Japanese attack targeted mainly military installations and personnel.

The LeT attack targeted only civilians — Indians and foreigners.

The ISI-sponsored LeT attack was as treacherous as the Japanese attack.

And as dastardly.

And how did we react?

As a nation?

As a people?

As a political class?

As we have always done.

Brave and indignant words in the beginning.

And a subsequent reluctance to translate the words into action.

The day of infamy on December 7, 1941, changed the history of the world.

And our own day of infamy of November 26, 2008?

Has it changed the history of the sub-continent?

Have we created the fear of God in the minds of Pakistan and its terrorist surrogates?

Have our reactions made it certain that there will not be another 26/11 in our history?

Far from it.

Far, far, far from it.

B. Raman
Chennai

ANOTHER DAY OF INFAMY

The war of civilization between the Muslims and the infidels has begun in Indian territory.

So said the first statement issued in the name of the so-called Indian Mujahideen (IM) in November, 2007, after three orchestrated explosions in three towns of Uttar Pradesh outside local courts.

We saw the latest round of this war in Mumbai from the night of November 26 to 29, 2008.

A group of 10 terrorists belonging to the Lashkar-e-Toiba (LeT) of Pakistan clandestinely sailed into Mumbai from Karachi in a hijacked Indian fishing trawler, landed in an inflated rubber dinghy in the darkness of early night, launched commando-style attacks in some sea front areas of the city and targeted with frightening precision two five-star hotels preferred by the rich of the country, foreign tourists and businessmen, a Jewish religious-cum-cultural centre, a railway station, a hospital and other places scattered across or near the sea front of this business capital of India.

It was not just 9/11. It was not just Madrid, March, 2004. It was not just London, July, 2005.

It was an act of terrorism the like of which the world had not seen before. It was a mix of a commando-style raid, typical of military special forces and terrorist attacks typical of the LeT. It was an operation conceived, planned and executed by a mix of military and terrorist brains.

The mind boggled as one tried to think and figure out how the terrorists could have planned and carried out terrorist strikes of such magnitude, territorial spread and ferocity without our intelligence and police having been able to get scent of it. Like what the Vietcong did during the Tet offensive in Vietnam.

Everyone connected with counter-terrorism in the Governments of India and Maharashtra was taken by surprise despite many indicators since November, 2007, that an iceberg of jihadi terrorism was on the move.

The iceberg moved from UP to Jaipur.

From Jaipur to Bangalore.

From Bangalore to Ahmedabad and Surat.

From there to Delhi.

It ultimately turned out that it was not this iceberg which hit Mumbai on November 26, 2008. It was a different iceberg, which moved directly from Karachi. Yet, in view of the repeated terrorist strikes in different parts of the country since the suburban train blasts in Mumbai in July, 2006, one would have expected the entire counter-terrorism machinery all over the country to have been in a heightened state of alert.

Particularly in Mumbai — which had seen two acts of mass casual terrorism originating from Pakistan in March, 1993 and in

July, 2006. Some of the Information Technology (IT) experts of the Indian Mujahideen had also been arrested in Mumbai. Despite this, every one responsible for counter-terrorism was caught napping once again.

It was not as if no intelligence was available. Intelligence agencies of India as well as the US had reportedly detected chatter in the jihadi circles in Pakistan about the plans of the LeT to attempt a sea-borne terrorist strike in Mumbai. The Taj Mahal Hotel, which was one of the two hotels attacked, had actually figured in the list of likely targets of the LeT.

Despite this, physical security, which is the basis of effective counter-terrorism, was found wanting.

Coastal surveillance and security against likely terrorist intrusions by sea was found wanting.

Alertness in the hotels attacked was found wanting.

The available intelligence might not have been complete in all respects, but it did provide a wake-up call, which was not heeded.

The Government of India had reacted to the repeated warning signals in the same way the Bush Administration had reacted to reports about the plans of Al Qaeda for an act of aviation terrorism in the US.

In the same way Megawati Sukarnoputri, former President of Indonesia, had reacted to reports about the activities of the Jemmah Islamiyah.

In the same way Khalida Zia, former Prime Minister of Bangladesh, had reacted to reports about the plans of the Jamiat-ul-Mujahideen to organize terrorist strikes in Bangladesh.

It just did nothing.

It was more interested in making peace with Pakistan than in protecting the lives and property of the people of India.

It was more interested in cultivating the so-called Muslim vote bank than in ensuring effective security for the citizens of India.

The country paid a heavy price for its inaction and ambivalence on the issue of terrorism.

One hundred and sixty-six persons — Indian civilians, brave officers and foreign nationals — paid with their lives for its inaction.

There was a big question mark over India's counter-terrorism capability. For the first time, questions were raised abroad about the ability of the Indian State to protect the lives and property of foreign nationals.

Hundreds of Indian civilians — men, women and children — had been killed by Pakistan-sponsored and aided terrorists since 1981, when terrorism made its appearance in India in a big way with the launching of the so-called Khalistan movement by a group of terrorists in Punjab.

But hardly less than 10 foreigners had been killed by terrorists of various hues during the long history of terrorism in Indian territory

— if one excludes the foreigners who died when the Babbar Khalsa blew up an aircraft of Air India (named Kanishka) off the Irish coast in June, 1985.

But more foreigners — 25 — were killed by the terrorists of the LeT in Mumbai between November 26 and 29, 2008, than the number killed by different terrorist organizations between 1981 and 2008.

It was a pre-planned and precisely executed attack on India.

It was an attack on India's business and financial capital.

It was an attack on foreign businessmen and investors who come to India to do business.

It was an attack on Israelis and other Jewish people who feel an instinctive sympathy for India because like India, Israel too has been a major victim of a jihadi terrorism of a brutal kind.

It was an attack on nationals of Western countries, which were involved in the war against Al Qaeda and the Taliban in the Pakistan–Afghanistan region.

According to the final investigation report submitted by the Mumbai Police to the trial court, the terrorists killed six from Israel, three each from the US and Germany, two each from Canada and Australia and one each from the UK, France, Belgium, Italy, Thailand, Singapore, Japan, Malaysia and Mauritius.

It was a brazen attack carried out without any regard for communications security. The 10 terrorists, who sailed from

Karachi to Mumbai to spread death and destruction, maintained communications with their controlling officers in Pakistan with their own telephones as well as with cellular phones, which they had seized from those held hostage by them. They were not worried over the dangers of their communications being intercepted.

They were not interested in ensuring the deniability of the Pakistani hand in the strike or of the identity of the LeT, which masterminded the attack. It was as if they wanted the entire world to know that a jihadi terrorist superstar has arrived.

As competent as Al Qaeda.

As well-motivated as Al Qaeda

As resourceful and innovative as Al Qaeda.

The world woke up with a shudder to the reality of the emergence of a new global terrorist organization, which could threaten international peace and security in the years to come.

Those who had been following the terrorist scene in Pakistan since 2002 would not have been surprised. There were enough indicators to warn that Al Qaeda was grooming the LeT to exercise the command and control of the global jihad since Al Qaeda found its movements and operational maneuverability restricted by the post 9/11 surveillance and security measures against it.

To share the leadership of the global jihad, Al Qaeda needed another organization about which the West knew little so that it could operate globally without major difficulties. The LeT footed the bill.

Till 2001, the West had looked upon the LeT as a purely Kashmir-centric organization, which threatened Indian lives and property, but not Western lives and property.

As a result, Western intelligence agencies paid very little attention to the LeT. Even the fact that Abu Zubaidah, the then No. 3 of Al Qaeda, was arrested from a safe-house of the LeT in Faislabad in Pakistani Punjab in March, 2002, did not sound a wake-up call in the West. "The LeT is India's headache, not ours." So they thought.

From 2003, sleeper cells of the LeT were discovered in the US, the UK, France, Australia and other countries. In subsequent months, there were traces of the LeT in Singapore. The LeT set up overseas bases in Saudi Arabia and Dubai to co-ordinate fund collection and its operations in India.

Still, the monitoring of the LeT received very low priority from the Western intelligence agencies.

But attitudes started changing after the London blasts of July, 2005. There was no evidence of any LeT involvement in the London blasts. But, the Pakistani suicide bombers, who carried out the blasts, had been trained in secret training camps in Pakistan.

Who trained them? Al Qaeda? The LeT? The Jaish-e-Mohammad? Nobody was certain. But almost all experts were convinced that a new brand of terrorists of Pakistani origin had started replacing the old brand of Arab terrorists, who spearheaded the pre-2005 global jihad.

It was no longer only the Salafis of the Arab world, who had to be feared. It was also the Wahabised Deobandis and Ahle Hadiths of Pakistan. It was their ideology emanating from mosques such as Binori in Karachi, which started motivating the post-9/11 global jihad.

We in India had known this for quite some time, but not the experts and policy-makers of the West. Our warnings regarding the pernicious nature of the LeT and the dangers it posed to the world were dismissed derisively as motivated by our dispute with Pakistan over Kashmir. The LeT was seen merely through the Kashmir prism.

But some started taking the LeT more seriously. They began seeing it as a global threat and not a threat directed merely at India.

The first evidence of this change in the attitude to the LeT was noticed at a special session on the London blasts organized during the annual conference of the Institute for Counter-Terrorism of Herzliya, Israel, in September, 2005. I was invited to be one of the speakers in the session. I could hardly believe my ears as I heard some of the speakers drawing attention to the dangers posed by the LeT.

On my return from Herzliya, I wrote as follows: "India is no longer alone in the fight against the LeT... Other countries of the world have been paying increasing attention to the activities of the pro-Al Qaeda Pakistani jihadi terrorist organizations such as the LeT, the Harkat-ul-Mujahideen (HuM), the Harkat-ul-Jihad-al-Islami (HUJI) and the Jaish-e-Mohammad (JeM) in Indian territory and their implications for their national security. This became evident during the fifth International Conference on the Global Impact of

Terrorism organized by the world-famous Institute for Counter-Terrorism (ICT) of Herzliya, Israel, from September 11 to 14, 2005. In his introductory remarks at the Panel on September 14, 2005, Mr. Shabtai Shavit, former Director-General of the MOSSAD, the Israeli external intelligence agency, made a reference to the activities of the LeT in the context of the international fight against Al Qaeda and Dr. Bruce Hoffman, who is considered the world's leading authority on Al Qaeda, inter alia, highlighted the role and the activities of the LeT during his presentation."

After 2005, the world was no longer unaware of the potential and threat of the LeT as a global terrorist organization following in the footsteps of Al Qaeda. But even this growing awareness had not prepared India and the rest of the world for the kind of complex, multi-target, multi-modus operandi commando style attack that the LeT carried out in Mumbai in November, 2008.

The world was surprised and shocked. So were we despite our extensive knowledge of the LeT.

The LeT's evolution from a sub-continental to a global jihadi terrorist organization was there for all the world to see as people saw with shock and disbelief live transmissions of the terrorist strikes on their TV screens with live commentaries by TV reporters.

THE EVOLUTION OF THE LeT
SINCE 2002

In a conversation with the editorial staff of the *Washington Post* on June 26, 2003, the then Pakistani President General Pervez Musharraf was reported to have claimed that he had effectively put an end to the terrorist activities of the LeT and the JeM, both members of Osama bin Laden's International Islamic Front (IIF), in Pakistan.

He was quoted as having told the newspaper's staff as follows: "The Lashkar-e-Toiba has been banned. The Jaish-e-Mohammad has been banned. There are hundreds of offices out there and I mean hundreds and hundreds of offices around the country, including Kashmir, have been sealed and closed. Their accounts have been frozen. Nobody before this could have touched them. They couldn't even have touched anyone of these organizations or their leaders."

The next day, as if to prove him wrong, the Federal Bureau of Investigation (FBI) charged seven men in the Washington area and an eighth in Philadelphia with stockpiling weapons and conspiring to wage "jihad" against India in support of a terrorist group in Kashmir. The FBI's charge-sheet against them described them as members of the LeT. It also said that three others involved in the case were absconding and were believed to be in Saudi Arabia.

Although the FBI officials said that there was no evidence of a plot against the US, the members of the group had pledged their support for pro-Muslim violence overseas, acquired high-powered rifles and received military training in Pakistan. Nine of the eleven accused were American citizens, and three had served in the US armed forces for some time in the past. The charge-sheet said that seven members of the group had travelled to Pakistan and some received military training in small arms, machine guns, grenade launchers and other weaponry at a camp in northeast Pakistan connected to the LeT.

The 41-count charge-sheet, or indictment as it is called in the USA, charged the 11 accused with conspiracy, firearms violations and plotting against a friendly nation — namely, India. US officials connected with the investigation were quoted by the media as saying that there was no evidence that the accused were considering an attack within the United States or had ties to Al Qaeda. And officials were careful not to describe the group as a "sleeper cell" — a term used to characterize suspected terrorist supporters in Lackawanna, N.Y., Seattle and elsewhere arrested in 2002, some of whom were connected with the Tablighi Jamaat (TJ) of Pakistan.

However, the officials charged that the men conspired to help Muslims abroad in violent jihad not only in India, but also in Chechnya, the Philippines and other countries. The men, the charge-sheet said, obtained AK-47s and other high-powered weaponry and practiced small-unit military tactics in Virginia.

The indictment charged that the accused pledged their willingness to die as martyrs in support of the Muslim cause and gathered in private homes and at an Islamic center in suburban Washington to hear lectures "on the righteousness of jihad" in Kashmir, Chechnya and elsewhere. They also watched videotapes showing Muslim fighters engaged in jihad. They had also organized a function to celebrate the crashing of the space shuttle *Columbia*. One of the astronauts killed in the crash was of Indian origin. A message read out on the occasion had described the USA "as the greatest enemy of the Muslims."

According to the indictment, one of the accused, Masoud Ahmed Khan, a Maryland resident, had a document titled *The Terrorist's Handbook*, with instructions on how to manufacture and use explosives and chemicals as weapons, as well as a photograph of the F.B.I. headquarters in Washington.

At least two of the 11 accused were described as of Pakistani origin. One of them, Mohammed Aatique, 30, was a work (H-1) visa holder while Khawja Mahmood Hasan, 27, was a naturalized US citizen born in Pakistan. But at least one more suspect, Masoud Ahmad Khan, 31, also had a Pakistani sounding name, although his nationality was not disclosed. The other accused were Randall Todd Royer, 30; Ibrahim Ahmed al-Hamdi, a Yemeni national and non-resident alien; Yong Ki Kwon, 27, a naturalized US citizen born in Korea; Seifullah Chapman, 30; Hammad Abdur-Raheem, 35; Donald Thomas Surratt, 30; Caliph Basha Ibn Abdur-Raheem, 29, and Sabri Benkhala, 28. Chapman, Hasan and Benkhala were said to be living in Saudi Arabia.

When an embarrassed Musharraf was asked about it at Los Angeles the next day, he was reported to have said: "We need to see who they are, where they were trained and how they were organized."

Earlier, on June 20, 2003, before the arrival of Musharraf in the

US for his Camp David meeting with the then President George Bush, FBI officials had disclosed that they had arrested in April Iyman Faris, also known as Mohammad Rauf, originally a resident of Pakistan-Occupied Kashmir (PoK), who had migrated to the US in 1994 and was working as a truck driver in Ohio. They charged him with having links with Al Qaeda and Khalid Sheikh Mohammad, said to be Osama bin Laden's operations chief, who is believed to have co-ordinated the terrorist strikes of September 11, 2001, in the US. Khalid was arrested in the house of a women's wing leader of the Jamaat-e-Islami (JeI) of Pakistan at Rawalpindi in March, 2003, by the Pakistani authorities and handed over to the FBI.

According to FBI officials, as quoted in the US media, Faris had visited Afghanistan and Pakistan a number of times between 2000 and 2002, met Osama bin Laden and worked with Khalid Sheikh Mohammad, in organizing and financing jihadi causes. After returning to the US from Pakistan in late 2002, officials said, he began examining the Brooklyn Bridge and discussing via coded messages with Al Qaeda leaders in Pakistan about ways of using blow torches to sever the suspension cables.

The plotting continued through March, as Faris sent coded messages to operatives in Pakistan. One such message said that the "weather is too hot". FBI officials believed that meant that Faris feared the plot was unlikely to succeed — apparently because of security and the bridge's structure — and should be postponed. He was arrested soon thereafter. According to media reports, the interrogation of Khalid led the FBI to Faris.

Around the same time, the US Homeland Security Department issued an alert to all airline companies about the dangers of a terrorist attack on the US Consulate in Karachi, mounted from the air. The staff of airline companies and airports were asked to be on the lookout for any suspicious attempts to hire trainer or other aircraft.

While there was no explanation for the issue of this alert, it came in the wake of the arrest of six persons said to be connected to Al Qaeda at Karachi on April 29, 2003. Three of these were described as hard-core members of Al Qaeda. They were Waleed Muhammad bin Attash alias Tawfiq bin Attash alias Khalid Al-Attash, described as a Yemeni suspect in the attack on the US naval ship USS *Cole* at Aden in October, 2000, Ali Abd al-Aziz also known as Ammar al-Baluchi — said to be a nephew of Khalid Sheikh Mohammad — and Abu Ammar. Aziz and Ammar were said to be Yemeni-Balochis.

Following these arrests, the Pakistani authorities issued their own alert, warning the local police and intelligence agencies to strengthen security measures to prevent any retaliatory attack on US nationals or establishments by Al Qaeda or its Pakistani associates in bin Laden's International Islamic Front (IIF).

What would appear to have caused the alarm was the recovery of a substantial quantity of explosives during the arrests. The circumstances, which led to the arrests, were not clear. According to one report, the Pakistan Rangers, during routine checking of suspect vehicles on the roads, found one carrying arms and ammunition and explosives. The interrogation of the driver of the vehicle led to an Al Qaeda hide-out in the Korangi area of Karachi, where more explosives were found and the other members were arrested. The collection of the explosives by the terrorists indicated that they were planning a major terrorist strike in Karachi, which had been prevented by their accidental arrest.

The Karachi Police were acting on the presumption that there must be other Al Qaeda hide-outs in Karachi, which had not so far come to notice and where more explosives might be stored. During previous arrests of Al Qaeda operatives in Pakistan, no explosives were found. However, explosives are available in plenty all over Pakistan and had been used in 2002 in the attack on some French submarine experts and in a car bomb explosion outside the US Consulate in Karachi.

In addition to these three Arabs, the Police also arrested three or more Pakistanis who were assisting them. The names of two of them were given as Muhammad Anwar alias Jabir and Habibullah alias Abdul Salam alias Imran. It was said that before coming to Karachi, they had participated in jihad in Afghanistan and in Jammu & Kashmir (J&K) in India.

During his interrogation by the Pakistani officials, Waleed was reported to have told them that in 2002 about 75 Arab operatives of Al Qaeda had fled from Afghanistan and the bordering areas of Pakistan and taken shelter at different places in Karachi. According to him, of these, about 50 were still in hiding in Karachi. He was also reported to have stated that he and his associates were recruiting Pakistani volunteers for undertaking suicide missions against American targets and that they had already recruited 12 persons from the LeT.

In the past, the LeT had kept its activities confined to its jihad in India and its assistance to the Jemmah Islamiyah and other pro-bin Laden elements in Indonesia. It did not utter any threats against the USA or target American nationals or interests. As a result, American intelligence officials based in Pakistan did not pay the same attention to monitoring its activities as they did to the activities of Al Qaeda and the other Pakistani organizations involved in the kidnapping and murder of Daniel Pearl, the US journalist, in January–February, 2002, and the murder of the wife and daughter of a US diplomat in an Islamabad church in March, 2002.

The LeT thus managed to retain its infrastructure and source of funding intact. Though it changed its name to Jamaat-ud-Dawa (JuD) to escape the consequences of the order banning it issued by Gen. Pervez Musharraf on January 15, 2002, it continued to be referred to by many Afghans, Pakistanis and Arabs as the LeT. Since the beginning of 2003, it was noticed trying to perform the role previously played by Al Qaeda as the coordinator of pro-bin Laden networks all over the world, as the supplier of funds to the networks in different countries and particularly in South-East Asia and of suicide volunteers, arms and ammunition and explosives to the surviving Al Qaeda operatives in Pakistan.

It reportedly re-organized its structure on the pattern of Al Qaeda and vastly expanded its activities in the business field in order to augment its sources of income. *The Friday Times* (January 17–23, 2003), the prestigious weekly of Lahore, reported as follows: "The Jamaat-ud-Dawa (JuD), formerly known as the Lashkar-e-Toiba, is snapping up properties across Pakistan. Sources told the weekly that recent real estate purchases by the JUD amount to about Rs. 300 million. It has reportedly bought four plots of land in the Hyderabad division (of Sindh) and six others in various Sindh districts. The total price tag is about Rs. 200 million. Recent purchases in Lahore have cost it Rs. 100 million." During the 2003 Eid festival in Pakistan, it was reported to have received charity contributions worth Rs. 710 million, mostly in the form of the hides of the sacrificed animals.

It was also in receipt of large funds from overseas Pakistanis. The annual report on the 'Patterns of Global Terrorism' during 2002 released to the media by the Counter-Terrorism Division of the US State Department on April 30, 2003, stated as follows on the LeT: "Collects donations from the Pakistani community in the Persian Gulf and United Kingdom, Islamic NGOs, and Pakistani and Kashmiri businessmen. The LT also maintains a Website (under the name of its parent organization, Jamaat ud-Daawa), through which it solicits funds and provides information on the group's activities. The amount of LT funding is unknown. The LT maintains ties to religious/militant groups around the world, ranging from the Philippines to the Middle East and Chechnya. In anticipation of asset seizures by the Pakistani Government, the LT withdrew funds from bank accounts and invested in legal businesses, such as commodity trading, real estate, and production of consumer goods." The State Department uses the abbreviation LT for the LeT.

In 2003, Al Qaeda was noticed trying to use the organizational infrastructure of the LeT in Pakistan, its network in the Islamic world and its large funds for stepping up acts of terrorism against the USA and Israel. Reports received during the year stated that the

LeT's close access to senior officers of the Pakistani military and intelligence establishment could be exploited by Al Qaeda to prevent any action against its surviving cadres in Pakistan. Many members of Pakistan's scientific community in the nuclear and missile fields regularly attended the conventions of the LeT. These reports said that by making use of this, Al Qaeda should be able to seek the assistance of LeT sympathizers in the scientific community for acquiring weapons of mass destruction expertise.

In an article of May 14, 2003, I wrote as follows: "The international community is yet to take serious notice of the emergence of the LeT as a coordinator of the activities of the various constituents of the IIF to make up for the present organizational disabilities of Al Qaeda. Next to Pakistan, where the headquarters of the LeT are located (in Muridke, near Lahore), the second most important infrastructure of the LeT is in Saudi Arabia. While the LeT's headquarters in Pakistan co-ordinate its activities in North India, including J&K, the Central Asian Republics (CARs) and Russia (Chechnya and Dagestan), its headquarters in Saudi Arabia co-ordinate its activities in Mumbai and South India, the Eastern Province of Sri Lanka and in the countries of S.E. Asia. Since 2001, there have been a number of arrests of LeT cadres in Mumbai and South India, who reportedly claimed to have been trained, funded and directed by the LeT set-up in Saudi Arabia and not directly by the LeT headquarters in Pakistan."

I wrote further: "Afghanistan–Pakistan–Saudi Arabia constitute a terrorism triangle. So-called charity and other private organizations in Saudi Arabia have been the generous providers of funds and volunteers for terrorist operations in different parts of the world;

the jihadi organizations of Pakistan have been the providers of sanctuaries, training, arms, ammunition and explosives and extra funds from the heroin trade; and Afghanistan was another provider of sanctuaries and training facilities, but this role has been reduced, if not eliminated, after the US air strikes on the training camps in Afghan territory. The Afghan-based terrorist infrastructure has since been transferred to Pakistani territory."

As a matter of policy, the LeT never claims responsibility for any acts of terrorism in the Indian territory outside J&K. Even in J&K, it claims responsibility only for attacks on the security forces and not for attacks on civilians. Its statements claiming responsibility are generally issued in the name of Zaki-ur-Rehman Lakhvi, who is designated as the supreme commander of the LeT. Pakistani sources describe Prof. Hafiz Mohammad Sayeed as the Amir of the Jamaat-ud-Dawa (JuD) and Lakhvi as the Amir of the LeT.

In an interview to *The Nation* (April 9, 1999) from Muzaffarabad, Zaki-ur-Rehman Lakhvi said: "We are extending our network in India and have carried out attacks on Indian installations successfully in Himachal Pradesh last year. To set up Mujahideen networks across India is our target. We are preparing the Muslims of India against India and when they are ready, it will be the start of the disintegration of India." Addressing a press conference at Muzaffarabad on March 2, 1999, Zafar Iqbal, the co-founder of the LeT, said that the LeT had invited Osama bin Laden to join the "freedom struggle" in Kashmir. He said that his organization would welcome bin Laden if he joined its struggle against the Indian army in Kashmir. He added: "Osama is our erstwhile colleague and we had fought jointly against the Soviet troops in Afghanistan."

Under US pressure following the terrorist strike on the Indian Parliament on December 13, 2001, Pervez Musharraf, in a telecast to his nation on January 12, 2002, announced his decision to ban the LeT and the Jaish-e-Mohammad (JeM). In pursuance of Musharraf's telecast announcement, Lt.Gen. (retd) Moinuddin Haider, Pakistan's then Interior Minister, issued a notification on January 15, 2002, formally banning the following five organizations under the Anti-Terrorism Act of 1997: the Lashkar-e-Toiba (LeT), the Jaish-e-Mohammad (JeM), the Sipah-e-Sahaba Pakistan (SSP), the Tehreek-e-Jafferia Pakistan (TJP) and the Tehreek-e-Nifaz-e-Shariat-e-Muhammadi (TNSM).The ban order was carried in the Pakistani Gazette the same day. The Gazette order banned the activities of the LeT only in Sindh, the Pakistani Punjab, the North-West Frontier Province (NWFP) and Balochistan. It did not ban its activities in the Federally-Administered Tribal Areas (FATA), the Northern Areas (NA) and PoK.

When Pakistani journalists questioned the local authorities about it, they were told that since the PoK was an autonomous State, only the local Government in Muzaffarabad had the power to issue a ban order. They also said that a separate ban order in respect of the FATA and the NA would follow. No ban order was issued by the PoK Government. Nor was any order issued by the Islamabad Government in respect of the FATA and the NA. Thus the legal position was that while the LeT could not operate in Sindh, Punjab, the NWFP and Balochistan, it was free to operate in the PoK, the

NA and the FATA. The Pakistani authorities also made it clear that the LeT and the JeM were being banned not because of the Indian allegations of their involvement in acts of terrorism in Indian territory, including Jammu & Kashmir (J&K), but because of their suspected terrorist activities in Pakistani territory.

1,957 persons belonging to the five banned organizations were detained and 615 of their offices sealed. Of them, 735 were detained and 336 offices sealed in Punjab; 852 arrested and 180 offices closed in Sindh; 337 detained and 81 offices shut in the NWFP; 15 arrested and an equal number of offices sealed in Balochistan; and 18 persons arrested and 3 offices closed in Islamabad. There was no action against their leadership, members and infrastructure in the FATA, the PoK and the NA. The majority of those arrested belonged to the political and administrative cadres of these organizations. There were practically no arrests of their trained terrorists. An estimated 5,000 trained terrorists were reported to have either escaped to the FATA, the PoK and the NA or gone underground in other parts of Pakistan. The trained terrorists of the LeT escaped to the PoK and the NA. Those of the JeM escaped to the FATA.

Among those arrested in Punjab was Prof. Hafeez Mohammad Sayeed, the Amir of of the Markaz Dawa Al Irshad (MDI), as the political wing of the LeT was then known. Lakhvi was not arrested. He shifted to the PoK and started operating from Shawai. At this camp, he used to train terrorists and send them into J&K and other parts of India for carrying out acts of terrorism. After some weeks, the Pakistani authorities released Sayeed and others arrested in the other provinces of Pakistan on the ground that investigations after their arrests did not find any evidence of their involvement in acts of terrorism in Pakistani territory. They rejected Indian allegations of their involvement in acts of terrorism in J&K and other parts of India. As regards their activities in J&K, they described them as part of a freedom struggle. As regards their activities in other parts of India, they asserted that India had not been able to produce any evidence in proof of its charge.

Sayeed re-named the MDI as Jamaat-ud-Dawa (JuD), a charity and humanitarian relief organization, which, according to him, had nothing to do with the LeT. The Pakistani media continued to identify the JuD as nothing but the LeT under a different name. Thus, two organizations started operating — the JuD headed by Sayeed in the four Pakistani provinces and the LeT headed by Lakhvi in the PoK and the NA. In his capacity as the Amir of the JUD, Sayeed started travelling all over Pakistan to collect funds and to set up the new network of the JuD.

Concerned over his activities, in 2004, the US again started pressing Musharraf to ban the JUD too and to enforce effectively the earlier ban on the LeT. The renewed US pressure was due to the following reasons:

- The unearthing of sleeper cells of the LeT in the USA and Australia.

- Its role in the training of a number of Indonesians and Malaysians, including the brother of Hambali of the Jemaah Islamiyah, in one of its madrasas in Karachi.

- Its suspected role in training some recruits from Singapore in one of its training camps in the PoK.

- Its assumption of the role of the coordinator of the International Islamic Front (IIF) formed by bin Laden in 1998.

- Its active role in collecting funds and recruiting volunteers for joining the jihad against the US troops in Iraq.

- The virulent anti-US statements in relation to Iraq issued by Prof. Sayeed.

- Reports circulating in Pakistan that Al Qaeda would in future be using non-Arab suicide volunteers recruited by the LeT in view of the difficulties faced by the Arab members of Al Qaeda in travelling to the US and other Western countries.

In the wake of the renewed US pressure came a report in the reliable *Daily Times* of Lahore (July 18, 2004) claiming that following personal differences with Sayeed over his marrying a 28-year-old widow, whose husband was killed in J&K, some members of the LeT had broken their links with the JuD and formed a new organization called the Khairun Naas, meaning "the Welfare of the Masses." The *Daily Times* reported as follows: "The Khairun Naas was established with the support of most of the Lashkar-e-Toiba and a majority within the party. The KN's leadership consists mostly of LeT commanders including Lakhvi, JUD Lahore head Abu Shoiab, Punjab head Abu Naser Javed, Abdul Qadir and Saifullah Mansoor. Prof Iqbal (Zafar Iqbal), publications chief Ameer Hamza, and JuD seminaries head Maulana Abdul Sallam Bhatvi are also supporting them. According to sources, Prof Iqbal is currently in Saudi Arabia seeking the support of Saudi clerics and the party's structure will be announced when he returns, probably with him at the top. Khairun Naas and Lashkar-e-Toiba are basically the same, but the LeT is banned in Pakistan so we adopted the name Khairun Naas," a member of the new party said. The sources said that the KN's claim to the LeT centre at Muridke was strong because of Mr Lakhvi. "Mr Lakhvi had close ties with the Arab Mujahideen and his sister was married to an Arab, Abdul Rehman Sherahi. It was Mr Sherahi who purchased the land on which the (Muridke) centre is built and gifted it to the JUD. Mr. Sherahi was arrested in Renala Khurd two years ago for connections with Al Qaeda. No one can claim the Muridke Markaz except Lakhvi, because it was established by his efforts," an aide of his said, the *Daily Times* reported. (*My comment*: According to reliable sources, the land at Muridke was actually given free of charge to the MDI by the late Zia-ul-Haq. The money for the construction of the centre was given by bin Laden and Sherahi. The Muridke centre used to have a guest house constructed for use by bin Laden during his visits to Muridke before 1992.)

A similar report was also carried by the *Herald,* the monthly of the Dawn group of publications. The *Herald* report identified Iqbal as the head of the KN. He and Sayeed had jointly founded the MDI and the LeT. Following this split, Maulana Ibrahim Salafi, a 56-year-old senior leader of the JUD, was shot dead in Lahore by unidentified persons on September 12, 2004. This gave rise to fears of a violent clash between the two groups. It was reported that Ayman al-Zawahiri, the No 2 to Osama bin Laden, sent for the representatives of the two groups and made them forget their differences and operate united once again under the leadership of Sayeed.

While the JUD, the LeT and the KN projected themselves as different organizations with no links to each other, sections of the Pakistani media treated all the three as one and the same. On April 27, 2006, the US State Department issued Executive Order 13224 designating the JUD as a terrorist organization and blocking property and interests in property, of the JUD and another linked organization, Idara Khidmat-e-Khalq, that are in the United States or the under the control of US persons. Earlier, in December 2001, the US had designated the LeT as a terrorist organization, but its attempt to persuade the monitoring committee of the UN Security Council to similarly designate the LeT could not succeed till May 2, 2005. During this period, Pakistan was a member of the monitoring committee, which monitors the implementation of the UN Security Council Resolution No.1373 against terrorism passed immediately after 9/11. All members of the UN Security Council are members of this monitoring committee, which acts on the basis of consensus. Pakistan resisted the US pressure to ban the JUD as a terrorist organization. It continued to assert that the JUD was a charity-cum-humanitarian relief organization and had nothing to do with the LeT.

A Pakistani Government spokesperson said on May 3, 2006: "The Government has no intention of designating the Jamaat-ud-Dawa and its affiliate organization as terrorist entities as done by the US. However, Pakistan would be legally bound to take action if they were placed on United Nations Security Council Sanctions Committee's consolidated list. The US had approached the UNSC for designation of the organizations as terrorist outfits and for putting them on the committee's list. We do not put any of our entities on the terrorist list if the action is taken under the US domestic law." Chinese support to the Pakistani contention that the JUD was not a terrorist organization and had no links with the LeT came in the way of the monitoring committee including the JUD in its list of terrorist organizations.

A press release of the US Department of Treasury issued on May 27, 2008, designated Sayeed, Lakhvi and two other office-bearers of the LeT as terrorists and highlighted their links with Al Qaeda. On August 14, 2008, Pakistan's Independence Day, the JUD held a conference in Lahore, called the "Defend Pakistan Conference." The conference opened with the singing by one Hafiz Abdul Wadud Hasan and Hafiz Abdur Rauf of what was described as the Jihadi National Anthem. The conference directed that in future this Anthem would be taught and sung in all training centres and madrasas controlled by the LeT.

The press release dated May 27, 2008, of the US Treasury Department said inter alia of the organization itself and of the four persons designated as terrorists as follows: "LeT is a dangerous al Qaida affiliate that has demonstrated its willingness to murder innocent civilians," said Stuart Levey, Under Secretary for Terrorism and Financial Intelligence (TFI). "LeT's transnational nature makes it crucial for governments worldwide to do all they can to stifle the LeT's fundraising and operations." LeT has conducted numerous attacks against Indian military and civilian targets since 1993. The Government of India implicated the LeT in the July 2006 attack on multiple Mumbai commuter trains, and in the December 2001 attack against the Indian Parliament. LeT is also suspected of involvement in attacks in New Delhi in October 2005, and in Bangalore in December 2005. In March 2002, senior al Qaida leader Abu Zubaydah was captured at an LeT safe house in Faisalabad, Pakistan. LeT arose in the early 1990s as the armed wing of the Sunni missionary movement Markaz-ud Dawa-wal-Irshad. Despite being banned by the Government of Pakistan in January 2002, LeT continues to operate in Kashmir and engage in or support terrorist activities worldwide. LeT was designated pursuant to US Executive Order 13224 on December 20, 2001, and under UN Security Council Resolution 1267 on May 2, 2005. The US Department of State named the LeT a Foreign Terrorist Organization (FTO) on December 26, 2001. Today's action was taken pursuant to Executive Order 13224, which targets terrorists and those providing financial, technological, or material support to terrorists or acts of terrorism. Any assets these designees have under US jurisdiction will be frozen and US persons are prohibited from engaging in any transactions with the designees."

The Press Release gave the following details of the four persons:

- Hafeez Mohammad Sayeed : He is the LeT's overall leader and chief and plays a key role in the LeT's operational and fundraising activities worldwide. He oversaw the management of a terrorist training camp in Pakistan in 2006, including funding of the camp, which prepared militants to fight against

Coalition forces in Afghanistan. In 2005, he determined where graduates of an LeT camp in Pakistan should be sent to fight, and personally organized the infiltration of LeT militants into Iraq during a trip to Saudi Arabia. That same year, he arranged for an LeT operative to be sent to Europe as the LeT's European fundraising coordinator.

- Zaki-ur-Rehman Lakhvi : He is the LeT's chief of operations. In this capacity, he directed LeT military operations, including in Chechnya, Bosnia, Iraq, and Southeast Asia. He instructed LeT associates in 2006 to train operatives for suicide bombings. Prior to that, he instructed LeT operatives to conduct attacks in well-populated areas. In 2004, he sent operatives and funds to attack US forces in Iraq. He also directed an LeT operative to travel to Iraq in 2003 to assess the jihad situation there. In past years, he also played an important role in LeT fundraising activities, reportedly receiving al Qaeda-affiliated donations on behalf of the LeT.

- Haji Muhammad Ashraf : He is the LeT's chief of finance, a position he has held since at least 2003. He traveled to the Middle East in 2003 and 2004, where he personally collected donations on behalf of the LeT. He assisted Saudi Arabia-based LeT leadership in 2003 with expanding its organization and increasing its fundraising activities.

- Mahmoud Mohammad Ahmed Bahaziq : A Saudi national. He is an LeT financier and is credited with being the main financier behind the establishment of the LeT and its activities in the 1980s and 1990s. He has also served as the leader of LeT in Saudi Arabia. In 2003, he coordinated the LeT's fundraising activities with Saudi non-governmental organizations and Saudi businessmen, and encouraged LeT operatives to continue and accelerate fundraising and organizing activities. As of mid-2005, he played a key role in the LeT's propaganda and media operations.

Earlier, a press note issued by the US Department of Treasury on October 16, 2003, designating Dawood Ibrahim, the Indian mafia leader living in Karachi under the alleged protection of the ISI, as a global terrorist indicated that the LeT was networking not only with Al Qaeda, but also with the gang of Dawood Ibrahim. It said: "Dawood Ibrahim, an Indian crime lord, has found common cause with Al Qaeda, sharing his smuggling routes with the terror syndicate and funding attacks by Islamic extremists aimed at destabilizing the Indian government. He is wanted in India for the 1993 Bombay Exchange bombings and is known to have financed the activities of the Lashkar-e-Tayyiba (Army of the Righteous), a group designated by the United States in October 2001 and banned by the Pakistani Government — who also froze their assets — in January 2002. Ibrahim's syndicate is involved in large-scale shipments of narcotics in the UK and Western Europe. The syndicate's smuggling routes from South Asia, the Middle East and Africa are shared with Osama bin Laden and his terrorist network. Successful routes established over recent years by Ibrahim's syndicate have been subsequently utilized by bin Laden. A financial arrangement was reportedly brokered to facilitate the latter's usage of these routes. In the late 1990s, Ibrahim travelled in Afghanistan under the protection of the

Taliban. Ibrahim's syndicate has consistently aimed to destabilize the Indian Government through inciting riots, acts of terrorism and civil disobedience. He is currently wanted by India for the March 12, 1993, Bombay Exchange bombings, which killed hundreds of Indians and injured over a thousand more. Information from as recent as Fall 2002, indicates that Ibrahim has financially supported Islamic militant groups working against India, such as the Lashkar-e-Tayyiba (LeT). For example, this information indicates that Ibrahim has been helping finance increasing attacks in Gujarat by the LeT."

A PRECURSOR TO NOVEMBER, 2008

One hundred and seventy-four persons were reported to have been killed in seven well-orchestrated explosions in Mumbai on July 11, 2006. Five of these explosions occurred in moving suburban trains and the remaining two in railway stations. Most of those killed and injured were railway commuters.

This was the third instance of mass casualty terrorism in the history of terrorism in India. The first was the blowing up of an aircraft (Kanishka) of Air India in June 1985 off the Irish coast by the Babbar Khalsa, a Sikh terrorist organization. About 300 innocent civilians were killed. The second was the Mumbai blasts of March, 1993, in which 250 innocent civilians were killed in 13 well-coordinated explosions directed against well-chosen economic targets by a group of Muslims trained and armed by the ISI, with the assistance of Dawood Ibrahim. The perpetrators were carefully selected Muslim youth, not belonging to any jihadi organization.

This was the fourth instance of co-ordinated serial blasts. The first was in June, 1985, when some Sikh terrorists placed transistor radio sets filled with small quantities of explosives in different parts of New Delhi. When passers-by picked up the radio sets and switched them on, the explosions took place. The casualties were small. The second was the Mumbai blasts of March, 1993, and the third the Coimbatore blasts of February, 1998, in which 33 people were killed and 153 others were injured in a series of 12 bomb blasts. The explosive material (RDX) used in March, 1993, was given to the perpetrators by the ISI. That used in February, 1998, was procured by the perpetrators locally.

This was the second instance of multiple explosions in trains. The first was carried out by the Students Islamic Movement of India (SIMI) in December, 1993, coinciding with the first anniversary of the demolition of the Babri Masjid in Ayodhya in Uttar Pradesh by a Hindu mob. Those were random explosions and not well-co-ordinated serial explosions. The casualties were small.

While in the past, the Pakistani pan-Islamic organizations and the ISI had taken advantage of the pockets of anger in the Indian Muslim community for their strategic objectives against India, since March, 2006, Al Qaeda had been trying to take advantage of them for its own pan-Islamic and anti-US objectives. The impact of Al Qaeda's propaganda and ideology on the minds of Indian Muslim youth, its possible inspiration behind the blasts of July 11, 2006, and likely threats to American interests in India from Al Qaeda started receiving some attention after the suburban train blasts. The Madrid blasts of March, 2004, were preceded by a strong anti-Spain propaganda by Al Qaeda. The London blasts of July 7, 2005, were preceded by a strong anti-UK propaganda by it. Anti-India statements of Al Qaeda since the visit of the then President George Bush to India in March, 2006 were not as virulent as its anti-Spain and anti-UK statements, but indicated the beginning of a new attention by Al Qaeda to India's developing relations with the US and Israel. In April, 2006, it started projecting India as a partner in the alleged US-Israeli conspiracy against the Muslims of the world.

The serial explosions of July 11, 2006, indicated continuing weaknesses in our national security management system. These weaknesses pertained to the preventive capability of our intelligence agencies, our physical security architecture and our crisis management capability.

The intelligence inadequacies were evident from our apparent failure to mount a vigorous drive to identify and neutralize sleeper cells which might have been operating in Mumbai following the recovery of explosives and other articles earlier in the year in the Aurangabad area.

The recovery of explosives should have set alarm bells ringing and led to a joint operation by the intelligence and security agencies of the Government of Maharashtra and the Centre for identifying terrorist networks, which might have escaped detection. If necessary, the other State police organizations should have also been associated with this. This was apparently not done. The whole thing seemed to have been treated in a casual manner.

The Special Task Force For the Revamping of the Intelligence Apparatus set up by the Government headed by AB Vajpayee in May, 2000, had, inter alia, recommended a number of measures to ensure better co-ordination in the collection of intelligence and in taking follow-up action relating to counter-terrorism. One of its recommendations for a multi-agency centre in New Delhi under the leadership of the Intelligence Bureau (IB) was quickly implemented. It consists of representatives of all agencies of the Government of

India dealing with terrorism and is headed by a senior officer of the IB. The Mumbai blasts of July, 2006, indicated possible inadequacies in its functioning. Another recommendation of the Task Force was for setting up a similar co-ordination mechanism in each State under the leadership of the IB. This recommendation had not been implemented by the Vajpayee Government till it left office. One had the impression after seeing what happened in Mumbai in July 2006 that there had been little progress in the implementation.

At a brain-storming session on national security management held in New Delhi in April, 2004, under the chairmanship of a very senior officer of the previous Government, I had referred to the lack of action to implement this recommendation. The senior officer replied: "Raman, you have no idea what difficulties I faced in making the agencies accept the recommendations relating to the Government of India. Where is the time and energy to attend to the recommendations relating to the State Governments?"

What follow-up action was taken after the recovery of the explosives? Was a general alert sounded to the police set-ups of all States? Was the public informed about it and its co-operation sought in looking for other consignments of explosives which might have been lying elsewhere? Were enquiries made about the origin of the explosives? The answers to these questions were not clear.

The Task Force for the Revamping of the Intelligence Apparatus mainly examined the inadequacies in the capabilities of the intelligence agencies for the collection of military intelligence regarding Pakistan as revealed by the Kargil conflict. It went into the counter-terrorism capabilities of the intelligence agencies only incidentally. Counter-terrorism was not one of its main terms of reference.

The Madrid blasts of March, 2004, and the London blasts of July, 2005, indicated the damage which the terrorists could cause to public transport systems, which were soft targets till then with very inadequate physical security.

These incidents led to an in-depth review in many countries of the world of the physical security set-up in public transportation systems in order to identify and plug loopholes. One cannot totally prevent terrorist attacks on public transportation systems, but one should be able to reduce the dangers of such attacks through enhanced physical security.

The Madrid and London blasts did not seem to have led to a similar review of physical security in our public transportation systems.

The weaknesses in our crisis management system were brought to light during the hijacking of an Indian Airlines plane to Kandahar by jihadi terrorists belonging to the Harkat-ul-Mujahideen in December, 1999.

It was alleged that even senior officers responsible for internal security were unaware of the crisis management drill to deal with hijackings which had been prepared in the 1980s and allowed the hijacked aircraft to take off from Amritsar, where it had initially landed, and to fly out of our air space.

From the kind of public complaints which one witnessed on TV after the 11/7 blasts, it was apparent that in the initial few hours the crisis management left much to be desired.

After the London blasts, the British Government had set up groups of experts to review the inadequacies in the intelligence collection, physical security and crisis management systems which came to light during the blasts and immediately thereafter and suggest correctives. No such action was taken by the Government of India after the July, 2006, blasts.

There was also an urgent need for an examination of the political and operational management of internal security tasks in the Ministry of Home Affairs of the Government of India. Till 1996, the two tasks were separated. While the Home Minister concentrated on the political management, he had under him a competent and live-wire Minister of State for Internal Security, who concentrated only on the operational management. In that capacity, he supervised intelligence collection, follow-up action, co-ordination between different agencies of the Government of India and between the Centre and the States, physical security and crisis management.

The post of Minister of State for Internal Security was held with great distinction by P Chidambaram under Rajiv Gandhi, Arun Nehru under VP Singh and the late Rajesh Pilot under PV Narasimha Rao. Since 1996, this division of responsibility for political and operational management has got blurred. The result: Political as well as operational management has suffered.

The seven serial explosions in Mumbai on July 11, 2006, were another wake-up call regarding the jihadi terrorists in our midst, whom we had not been able to detect and neutralize.

Many terrorist cells had been detected and put out of action by our intelligence and security agencies in the past, but, unfortunately, the more we kill or capture, the more the flow of new recruits to their cause. Their motivation and determination to keep up the jihad against the Indian State and society remain strong.

While testifying before the US Congress in 2005, a senior US counter-terrorism expert said: "We know what we know, but we don't know what we don't know".

That is the dilemma of counter-terrorism. One knows how many cells one has put out of action, but one does not know how many still remain undetected, waiting to strike at a time and place of their choosing.

Mumbai-11/7 showed that well-motivated cells, with well-motivated cadres continue to be available in Mumbai for jihadi terrorist strikes. Two organizations had operated with some success in Mumbai in the past — the Students' Islamic Movement of India (SIMI) and the LeT

One could, therefore, conclude that one or both these organizations must have had a hand in organizing the explosions, but the sophistication of the planning and execution of the blasts indicated guidance and inspiration from Al Qaeda, but a possible Al Qaeda angle behind the LeT was played down during the investigation for political reasons. No political leader in the so-called secular parties was prepared to draw attention to the possibility of pro-Al Qaeda extra-territorial loyalties in some elements of our Muslim community.

It would have been difficult to plan in secrecy and carry out successfully the kind of terrorist strikes seen on July 11, 2006, without local support in the Muslim community in the form of logistics, sanctuaries for stay and places of storage for the explosives.

It was very likely that members of the local Muslim community were aware of the movement of men and material in connection with the blasts, but apparently they did not alert the police either due to fear of retaliation by the terrorists or due to sympathy for them.

After the March, 1993 serial blasts too, one felt that some members of the local Muslim community were aware of the clandestine landing of explosives, detonators, timers and hand-grenades at different points on the coast, but they did not alert the police.

The March, 1993, explosions in Mumbai showed that while our intelligence and security agencies were strong in their ability to investigate a terrorist strike, identify those responsible and arrest and prosecute them, they were weak in their ability to prevent it.

Thirteen years later, the position had improved as indicated by the number of cells detected and neutralized and the number of terrorist strikes thwarted. At the same time, the fact that successful terrorist strikes, some of them serious, continued to take place showed enduring weaknesses in our preventive capability.

Recruitment from the Indian Muslim community, which

remained a trickle in the 1990s, has picked up momentum in recent years. The pan-Islamic ideology of Al Qaeda had no takers even among the alienated sections of the Indian Muslim community in the past. However, since March, 2006, Al Qaeda has stepped up its efforts to promote a trend towards the pan-Islamisation of the Indian Muslim youth.

In cautiously-worded remarks after a visit to Mumbai on July 14, 2006, the Prime Minister, Dr Manmohan Singh, was quoted as saying with reference to the likely Pakistani role in the multiple terrorist strikes of July 11: "The terrorists behind Tuesday's serial blasts in Mumbai were supported by elements across the border. Without the support from elements across the border, the terrorists would not have been able to carry out strikes with such an effect."

He did not name Pakistan, but it was obvious who he had in mind. During his meeting with AB Vajpayee, the then Indian Prime Minister, at Islamabad in January, 2004, Musharraf gave a formal assurance that he would not allow the use of Pakistani or Pakistani-controlled territory for acts of terrorism against India. The expression 'Pakistani territory' referred to Punjab, Sindh, Balochistan, the North-West Frontier Province (NWFP) and the Federally-Administered Tribal Areas (FATA) and 'Pakistani-controlled' territory to Pakistan-Occupied Kashmir (PoK) and the Northern Areas (Gilgit and Baltistan).

The Government of Pakistan and the jihadi organizations controlled by it have been following a dual policy with regard to jihadi terrorism in Indian territory. They denied that what was happening in Jammu & Kashmir (J&K) amounted to terrorism. Instead, they projected it as a justified "freedom struggle". The Government of Pakistan did not deny that it was giving political, diplomatic and moral support to this "freedom struggle", but denied giving it any material support in the form of funds, training, arms and ammunition and operational guidance. The Pakistani jihadi terrorist organizations made no secret of their role in assisting this "freedom struggle". They did not hesitate to claim credit for their operations in J&K.

With regard to acts of jihadi terrorism in Indian territory outside J&K, the Government of Pakistan always condemned it as terrorism and did not try to project it as a "freedom struggle". The Pakistani jihadi organizations did not condemn them as acts of terrorism, but denied any role in those acts. At the same time, they expressed their moral and religious support to their co-religionists in Indian territory who, according to them, were fighting for their "liberation" from Hindu domination.

Even before Gen Musharraf's commitment to Vajpayee in January, 2004, one had noticed two significant changes in the activities of the Pakistani jihadi terrorist organizations operating in Indian territory. First, there was a drop in acts of Pakistani-sponsored jihadi terrorism in Indian territory outside J&K. There was no major act of jihadi terrorism in the Indian territory outside J&K between September, 2003, and July, 2005. This was attributable to two reasons. A Pakistani decision to keep the operations of the organizations sponsored by it confined to J&K and successful preventive actions by the Indian intelligence, which detected and neutralized many sleeper cells in different parts of the country.

Second, the Pakistani organizations operating in J&K started concentrating on attacking the security forces and their political masters and avoided attacking civilians. There were instances of civilian deaths as collateral damage, but very few targeted attacks on civilians. This change was probably motivated by the bad name which Pakistan was getting from the international community.

There was a reversal of this policy from July, 2005. Pakistani organizations resumed their acts of terrorism in the Indian territory outside J&K from July 5, 2005, when they unsuccessfully attacked a Hindu temple at Ayodhya in Uttar Pradesh. This was followed by the twin explosions in a shopping area of New Delhi in October, 2005, in which 59 civilians were killed, the attack on the participants in a conference of scientists at Bangalore in December, 2005, resulting in the death of one scientist, the explosions in Varanasi, the Hindu holy town, in March, 2006, and the Mumbai attack of 11/7, which was the most serious and well-organized targeted attack on civilians since the March, 1993 explosions in Mumbai.

Simultaneously, the Pakistani jihadi organizations resumed their policy of targeted attacks on civilians in J&K — tourists from other parts of India, Hindus in the Jammu area, etc. Interestingly, this period also saw the ISI resuming its assistance to the Taliban and Gulbuddin Heckmatyar's Hizbe Islami to enable them to stage a come-back in Afghanistan.

Why this reversion to the pre-September, 2003, practice of

the use of the jihadi weapon against India and Afghanistan? Two explanations were available from an analysis of reports from reliable Pakistani sources and Pakistani media reports. Firstly, an assessment by the Corps Commanders of the Pakistani Army in June 2005 that the non-use of the jihadi sword could result in the de facto status quo in J&K and Afghanistan becoming a de jure reality. They felt this would be detrimental to Pakistan's interests.

Secondly, Musharraf's need of the assistance of the jihadi organizations to defeat the attempts of Mrs Benazir Bhutto's Pakistan People's Party Parliamentarians and Nawaz Sharif's Pakistan Muslim League to win the general elections of 2008. In the elections of October, 2002, Musharraf used the fundamentalist organizations, which contested the elections, and the jihadi organizations, which worked in the field without contesting the elections, to defeat the candidates of the parties of Mrs Bhutto and Sharif. The result: the coming to power of the fundamentalist parties in the NWFP and Balochistan. This gave a fillip to the activities of the remnants of Al Qaeda and the Taliban, which enjoyed the support of the ruling dispensation in these two key provinces.

It was reported that Musharraf had asked the ISI to give the jihadi organizations all the assistance they needed for their operations in India and Afghanistan in return for their support to him and the parties controlled by him in the elections. He also ordered the suspension of all action against madrasas, which were training foreign jihadis.

One should underline some disturbing indicators relating to our counter-terrorism capability, prevention and investigation, which were noticed post-July, 2006. It was evident that the suburban railway system in Mumbai had very little physical security. The terrorists had noticed this, but not our national security managers at the central and state levels.

What were the reported facts? On an average, generally, each railway station had four constables to ensure its security. There were days when due to sickness and other reasons, even these four constables were not posted and the stations had no security cover. There was no closed circuit TV and no anti-explosive check through door-frame metal detectors and sniffer dogs. The Railway Protection Force (RPF) in Mumbai had four trained dog squads. These were employed for anti-explosive checks in long-distance trains only. Whatever little physical security was there seemed to have been based on the assumption that the terrorists were more likely to attack long-distance trains than suburban trains. One did not know on what basis the security of the commuters by suburban trains was neglected.

The second disturbing indicator related to forensic examination of the scenes of the terrorist attacks, particularly the railway compartments in which the explosions took place. Normally, in any investigation done in a professional manner, the first step is to identify the place where the explosive device was placed, isolate it and mount a guard till forensic experts have thoroughly examined the place and gathered all evidence of forensic value. One had the impression that this was not done for some hours. As a result, there seemed to have been considerable disturbance of the scenes of the blasts by police and railway staff, humanitarian workers and other curious on-lookers. The disturbance was apparently so bad that experts in explosives could not even get adequate samples from the blown up compartments by examining which they could have determined the nature of the explosive. As a result, there was some delay and avoidable confusion in determining the nature of the explosive used.

The third disturbing indicator was about the investigation into the case relating to the discovery of over 40 kilos of RDX explosive by the Police in May, 2006, in the Aurangabad area. Some local Muslims were arrested by the police in this connection, kept in police custody and then sent to judicial custody after interrogation. The police had a second look at this investigation in order to see whether they might have contained clues about the explosions of 11/7, which they might have missed at that time. Going back into past cases in order to look for missed clues is part of the investigation process.

But one got the impression that despite questioning about 12 persons allegedly involved in the transport of the explosives in May, 2006, the police could not establish where they brought the explosives from, in which quantity, were there other quantities stored elsewhere, by whom, etc.

One saw a certain disturbing pattern being repeated after every jihadi terrorist strike — excitement all around, names of alleged suspects being disseminated through the kindness of willing journalists, a plethora of theories — some plausible, some fanciful — raids into the houses of likely suspects here and there, claims of major break-through and then silence, with nothing more said or apparently done about the investigation.

A similar thing happened in respect of Mumbai-11/7. In the newspapers, it disappeared quickly from the front pages. The new theme of excitement for the TV channels was what Israel was doing in Lebanon — should India emulate Israel? Less and less analysts discussed the progress of the investigation and posed inconvenient questions to the police and our national security managers.

Within a few weeks of July, 2006, we were back to our normal state of excitement — with more time, column space and prime time being spent on the progress in the Congressional approval of the India–US nuclear deal than in the investigation of the Mumbai blasts. We were more preoccupied with the nuclear and other so-called strategic issues and discussing vigorously how should India play its role as an emerging global power, without worrying about our chronic inability to ensure effective internal security.

The political leaders were back to their basics — calling each other names, accusing each other of incompetence, blaming each other for being soft. Pots continued to call the kettles black. In the meanwhile, the terrorists continued to strike at regular intervals here, there and everywhere. They continued to have the last laugh.

I wrote after the Mumbai blasts of July, 2006: "It is time the Central Government starts exercising a vigorous leadership role in strengthening our counter-terrorism capabilities — prevention through timely intelligence and effective physical security, deterrence through thorough investigation and prosecution leading to convictions and mobilizing the people through a national consensus. How can our political leaders mobilize the people and motivate them to join hands in the fight against terrorism when they cannot mobilize and motivate themselves to join hands? Whether we admit it or not, Al Qaeda has arrived in India — not as an organization, but as an ideology, as a source of inspiration and sophisticated modus operandi, as the puller of the jihadi strings from its bases in Waziristan in Pakistan. Jihad in India has started becoming part of the global jihad. More Mumbais are likely if we do not draw the right lessons and start acting vigorously against the new jihadi terrorism."

Our failure to admit and address the sins of commission and omission of July, 2006, inexorably led to Mumbai, November, 2008.

MUMBAI 26/11 — AN OVERVIEW

In 2008, India faced six major acts of terrorism in Indian territory outside J&K. Of these, four in Jaipur (May), Bangalore (July), Ahmedabad (July) and Delhi (September) were committed by some members of the Students' Islamic Movement of India (SIMI), which has had contacts with the LeT. In messages sent before and after the attacks, they described themselves as the Indian Mujahideen (IM). The IM came to notice for the first time in November 2007 when it organized three explosions in three towns of Uttar Pradesh. In a message sent to sections of the media that day, it accused the Indian criminal justice system of being unfair to Muslims. All these four were acts of reprisal terrorism with no strategic objective.

During these strikes, the IM did not attack foreigners either in Jaipur, which has the second largest foreign tourist traffic after Goa or in Bangalore, which is one of the favourite destinations for foreign business companies.

India has been facing terrorist attacks by home-grown jihadi groups since 1993. The defining characteristics of these attacks were:

- No suicide or suicidal (fedayeen) terrorism. No Indian Muslim has so far indulged in suicide terrorism in Indian territory. The only instance of suicidal terrorism by an Indian Muslim was in Glasgow in UK in June, 2006.

- No barbaric methods such as slitting the throats of the victims. Such barbaric methods are the signature modus operandi of jihadis from Pakistan.

- Reliance more on improvised explosive devices (IEDs) than on hand-held weapons.

- No attacks on foreign nationals except once in 1991 when the J&K Liberation Front (JKLF) killed one Israeli tourist in Srinagar.

Of the remaining two terrorist strikes in 2008, one in Assam in October was committed by a local ethnic group with the help of elements from Bangladesh and the other in Mumbai in November by 10 Pakistani members of the LeT.

The defining characteristics of the Mumbai attack were:

- This was the first attack of suicidal (fedayeen) terrorism in the Indian territory outside J&K. All previous fedayeen attacks were in J&K.

- This was the second attack in Indian territory outside J&K in which all the principal perpetrators were Pakistani nationals. The first one was the attack on the Indian Parliament on December 13, 2001.

- This was the second attack of jihadi terrorists on India's economic infrastructure. The first was in March, 1993 — also in Mumbai.

- The LeT terrorists attacked a mix of targets — human beings as well as economic capabilities, the man in the street as well as the elite and Indians as well as foreigners.

- This was the first attack by jihadi terrorists on foreigners in Indian territory outside J&K. Since 9/11, there have been 13 targeted attacks on foreigners in the Indian sub-continent — 12 in Pakistani territory and the Mumbai one in Indian territory. Of the 12 attacks in Pakistani territory, five were on Chinese nationals, four on American nationals and one each on French, German and Danish nationals or interests.

- This was the first terrorist attack on Israelis and the Jewish people in the Indian territory outside J&K. It came in the wake of intelligence warnings that the LeT and the SIMI were planning to attack Israeli tourists in Goa. Khalid Sheikh Mohammad had reportedly told his American interrogators that Al Qaeda had wanted to attack the Israeli Embassy in New Delhi. Mumbai has two establishments associated with Israel and the Jewish people — the Israeli Consulate and the Narriman House. The terrorists came by sea and attacked at night. They chose the Narriman House and not the Consulate because it is near the sea and had Jewish people living there, whereas the Consulate has no Jewish people at night.

- There was a mix of modus operandi (MO) — urban warfare of the kind waged by the Hezbollah in Beirut and orchestrated acts of mass casualty terrorism of the kind waged by Al Qaeda; and old terrorism involving the use of hand-held weapons, hand-grenades and explosives and new terrorism involving the use of the latest communications and navigation gadgetry. The TV visuals from Mumbai during the 60 hours that the attack lasted brought back to the minds of professionals visuals, which used to come out of Beirut.

- There was a mix of strategies — a strategy for disrupting the Indo-Pakistan peace process was combined with a strategy for acts of reprisal against India's close relations with Israel and the West. A strategy for discrediting the Indian counter-terrorism community and policy-makers in the eyes of the Indian public was combined with a strategy for discrediting them in the eyes of the international community and business class.

- There was a mix of attacks on the man in the street in public places such as a railway station, a public square, a hospital, etc and on the business and social elite in the Taj Mahal and the Oberoi/Trident Hotels. These are not ordinary hotels patronized by tourists who travel on a shoe-string budget. These are very expensive hotels patronized by the cream of the international business class, who visit Mumbai not for pleasure, but for business.

- The terrorists did not indulge in classical hostage-taking tactics, where one takes hostages in order to put forward a demand. They took hostages and locked themselves in buildings in order to force an armed confrontation with the security forces.

- The grievances of the Indian Muslims were not the cause of the terrorist attack. Pakistan's strategic objectives against India, such as forcing a change in the status quo in J&K and disrupting

India's economic progress and strategic relations with the West and Israel were the principal motive.

• Reprisal against the US-led coalition in Afghanistan for its war against Al Qaeda and the Taliban was another motive.

There was considerable criticism of the Indian counter-terrorism community — some justified and some unfair. In September, 2008, there were reports from the Indian and US intelligence that LeT terrorists in Pakistan were planning to carry out a sea-borne terrorist strike against sea-front hotels in Mumbai, including the Taj Mahal hotel. A high-alert was issued. Security was tightened by the Police, the Navy, the Coast Guard and the security set-ups of the hotels. The terrorists, who had planned to strike on September 26, postponed their attack. There was no fresh information in October. No terrorist strike came. The alert was reportedly downgraded in November. The attack came on November 26. It is always a dilemma for the counter-terrorism community as to for how long should a high alert be continued.

There was also criticism of what was described as the slow response of India's special intervention forces, such as the National Security Guards (NSG). While some Western analysts criticized their response as too slow taking about 60 hours, some Israeli analysts criticized it as too hasty, without trying to tire the terrorists out by indulging in talks with them. The NSG did not have the luxury of many options since it was not a classical hostage situation. Their objective was to save as many lives as possible from three different places which were under the control of the terrorists.

There are two ways of assessing the performance of the NSG and the Police. The first is from the number of people killed by the terrorists in these three places — about 100. The second is from the number of people, whom they rescued alive — nearly 1000. Let us applaud them for saving so many people despite the difficulties faced by them.

The most objective assessment of the performance of the NSG and the Police came from Ami Pedazhur, a professor of Middle Eastern studies at the University of Texas at Austin, and the author of the forthcoming book *The Israeli Secret Services and the Struggle Against Terrorism*. In an article contributed by him to the *New York Times* (December 19, 2008), Pedazhur wrote: "It is clear that the Indian security forces made some mistakes. However, mistakes are inherent in such crises. At the same time, given the complex nature of the attacks, it seems likely the death toll could have been much higher. After the initial confusion, the Indians seem to have done a thorough job of gathering intelligence and carefully planning their counter-attacks. The execution itself was careful and thorough."

He added: "The Mumbai attacks showed just how difficult it is for large, multi-ethnic states to protect themselves from terrorism, something Americans have known well since 9/11. There is certainly much for New Delhi and Washington to learn from the Israeli experience, but there is no one-size-fits-all solution. While Israel has much to be proud of in how it has handled terrorism, it also has much to be humble about."

Counter-terrorism is much more difficult in India than in any other country because of its large size, federal constitution which gives greater powers to the State governments in respect of crime control and law and order, multi-party system and coalition governments at New Delhi and in many States. Moreover, India is located right in the centre of the Islamic world with Islamic countries to the East, West and North-West of it. It has the second largest Muslim population in the world after Indonesia. Actions against jihadi terrorists — whether home-grown or externally sponsored — have to be attentive to the sensitivities of the Muslim community while acting against the terrorist elements from them. This often creates a Hamlet-like situation for the counter-terrorism community. Political consensus on counter-terrorism related issues is more difficult to achieve than in other democracies.

Certain facts available should give an idea of the magnitude of the terrorist strikes, the like of which the world had not seen before:

- There were 13 incidents of intense firing with assault rifles at different places, including the Chhatrapati Shivaji Train (CST) terminus, the Metro Cinema junction, the Cama and Albless Hospital, outside the Olympia restaurant in Colaba, the lobbies of the Taj Mahal and Oberoi/Trident hotels, and the Leopald Café behind the Taj Mahal Hotel.

- Near the Metro Cinema junction, some terrorists hijacked a police vehicle and went around spraying bullets on passers-by.

- There were seven incidents involving explosive devices — outside the Taj Mahal Hotel, in the BPT Colony at Mazgaon, three near the Oberoi/Trident Hotels, the Colaba market and inside a taxi.

- There were some incidents of throwing hand-grenades — two of them at the Cama hospital and on Free Press Road.

- There were three incidents of fidayeen style (suicidal, not suicide) infiltration into buildings followed by a prolonged confrontation with the security forces before being killed. These took place in the Taj Mahal and the Oberoi/Trident hotels and in the Narriman House in Colaba, where a Jewish religious-cum-cultural centre is located, headed by a Jewish Rabbi. Jewish people of different nationalities often congregate there. The centre also has cheap accommodation for Jewish visitors from abroad.

- According to the local authorities, most of the hotel guests who were subsequently rescued by the National Security Guards (NSG) had run into their rooms and locked themselves up when the terrorist forced their way into the lobbies and restaurants and started opening fire. They were not hostages.

- However, the terrorists took six Jewish people hostages in Narriman House. They were found dead when the NSG made their entry and killed the terrorists. It was not known how they died — through bullet wounds or beheading as the jihadis normally do.

- Almost all the terrorist strikes took place against targets near the sea. The terrorists did not venture out into the interior.

Governmental experts played down the possibility of an Al Qaeda inspiration despite tell-tale signs of an Al Qaeda stamp on the strikes. They continued to maintain a silence on the possible role of sections of the Indian Muslims lest any open projection of this cost them Muslim votes. They highlighted the role of the LeT, but without drawing attention to the fact that it is a member of Osama bin Laden's International Islamic Front (IIF) and that it had many associates in the Indian Muslim community.

The Prime Minister was unwise in reportedly suggesting or welcoming a visit to India by Lt.Gen. Ahmed Shuja Pasha, the Director-General of Pakistan's Inter-Services Intelligence (ISI), for discussions on the Mumbai attack. One fails to understand what useful results would have come out of it. By failing to act against the LeT, its leaders and terrorist infrastructure even after ostensibly banning it on January 12, 2002, the State of Pakistan had definitely facilitated its acts of terrorism in Indian territory. By sharing the information collected by us at that stage with the ISI chief, we would have helped him in covering up the tracks of the LeT and the ISI before we could complete the investigation. The visit fortunately did not materialize as there was opposition to it in Pakistan, particularly from the Army.

One should not be surprised if the suggestion for the visit had come from the US and the Prime Minister had accepted it just as he reportedly accepted in September, 2006, the US suggestion for setting up a joint counter-terrorism mechanism with Pakistan. The American ploy would have been to divert any Indian public anger away from Pakistan and the Prime Minister should have firmly rejected it.

Three of the most gruesome acts of terrorism since India became independent have taken place in Mumbai — the March 1993 blasts, the July 2006 blasts in suburban trains and the strikes of November, 2008. It is a shame that we have not been able to protect this city effectively, which is the jewel of India. Mumbai is India's New York and Shanghai. Look at the way the Americans have protected NY after 9/11. Look at the way the Chinese have protected Shanghai. The immediate priority of the Government should have been to set up a joint task force of serving and retired officers from Maharashtra in the Police, intelligence agencies and the Armed Forces to work out and implement a time-bound plan to ensure that 26/11 cannot be repeated again. Mumbai has till now been the gateway of India. The terrorists have exploited it. We should make it Fortress India. Foreign investors will lose confidence in India if Mumbai, where many of the corporate headquarters are located, can be attacked repeatedly with impunity by terrorists.

The second lesson was that confidence-building measures with Pakistan should not be at the expense of national security. In the name of confidence-building, there have been too many relaxations of immigration regulations applicable to Pakistan. There has been pressure on the Government for more relaxations from the so-called Indians–Pakistanis Bhai Bhai (Indians–Pakistanis are brothers) lobby. The terrorists have been a major beneficiary of these relaxations. These relaxations have decreased the vigilance of our people. For example, hotels, which immediately used to alert the Police when a Pakistani national or a foreigner of Pakistani origin checked in, no longer do so.

The use of boats and dinghies for the clandestine transport of men and material for terrorist strikes on land is an old modus operandi (MO) used in the past against Israel. The Liberation Tigers of Tamil Eelam (LTTE) had copied it from them. The anti-India jihadis emulated their West Asian counterparts.

The use of boats for transport enables the terrorists to evade physical security checks by road, rail and air. The numerous creeks between India and Pakistan across the Bhuj area of Gujarat enable the ISI and the pro-Al Qaeda Pakistani terrorist organizations to clandestinely transport men and material by sea. Reports that the ISI had planned to use this MO for helping the Khalistani terrorists in the 1990s had led to the Border Security Force acquiring some boats which could be used for surveillance in these creeks.

The success of the terrorists in evading detection by our Coast Guard and the police revealed a serious gap in our maritime counter-terrorism architecture. If this gap is not quickly identified and closed, the vulnerability of the Bombay High off-shore oil installations and the nuclear establishments to terrorist attacks from the sea would be increased. Many of our nuclear and space establishments — not only in Mumbai, but also in other areas — are located on the coast and are particularly vulnerable to sea-borne terrorist attacks.

The stamp of Al Qaeda was evident in the selection of targets. The Taj Mahal Hotel, old and new, the Oberoi-Trident Hotel and the Narriman House were the strategic focus of the terrorist operation. The terrorist strikes in other places such as the railway station, a hospital, etc and instances of random firing were of a tactical nature intended to create scare and panic.

The strategic significance of the attacks on the two hotels from

Al Qaeda's point of view arose from the fact that these hotels are the approved hotels of the US and Israeli Governments for their visiting public servants and for the temporary stay of their consular officials posted in Mumbai till a regular house is found for them. These hotels are also the favorites of the foreign business elite visiting or living in Mumbai.

Al Qaeda and pro-Al Qaeda organizations have been critical of India's close co-operation with Israel and the US. In the past, the ISI had also shown an interest in having Indo–Israeli relations disrupted through terrorist attacks on visiting Israeli nationals in India. In 1991, it had instigated an attack by the Jammu & Kashmir Liberation Front on some Israeli tourists in Srinagar by alleging that they were really Israeli counter-terrorism experts.

The attacks on the foreigners in the hotels were selective and not indiscriminate. Available reports indicated that the terrorists were looking for American, British and Israeli nationals — particularly visiting public servants among them with official or diplomatic passports.

According to the *Hindustan Times* (December 2, 2008), the LeT's name as the main plotter of a sea-borne terrorist strike in Mumbai directed against some sea front hotels figured in three technical intelligence reports of the Research & Analysis Wing (R&AW) based on intercepts reportedly of September 18, September 24 and November 19, 2008. These reports were more specific than the earlier interrogation reports about terrorist strikes planned in Goa. However, whereas the reports relating to Goa spoke specifically of Israeli and Western tourists as the targets, the R&AW reports, while indicating that the sea-side hotels in Mumbai preferred by foreign tourists would be the targets, did not speak specifically of Israeli and Western tourists. Nor was there any reference to a planned terrorist strike in Narriman House. Among the hotels reportedly mentioned by the R&AW was the Taj Mahal Hotel.

The presence of the Jewish centre in the Narriman House was not very well known in Mumbai outside Jewish circles. The fact that the terrorists had come to know about it and had included it as one of their principal targets spoke of their extensive local knowledge and of the enquiries that must have been made by them about Israeli/Jewish offices and places of stay near the sea front. They must have made detailed local enquiries either during an advance visit or through accomplices in the local Muslim community. The knowledge, which they seem to have had about the Narriman House, definitely spoke of some local involvement at least in intelligence collection. Mark Sofer, the Israeli Ambassador to India, was quoted as saying: "Out of the thousands of buildings in Mumbai, it was hard to believe that the terrorists had stumbled by chance upon the Jewish center." They did not target the local Israeli Consulate.

They wanted to kill as many Jewish people as possible and this might not have been possible in the five-star hotels because most Israeli tourists come on a shoe-string budget and stay in cheap hotels away from the sea front. The Narriman House provided a point where many Jewish people — locals, Israelis and Jewish visitors from other countries — congregate. However, since they attacked the place around 10 PM, not many Israelis and other Jewish people were present there. They were able to get only six Jewish people living or temporarily staying in the premises.

The terrorists did not appear to have been interested in taking the Jewish people as hostages and using them to achieve any demand. They just wanted to torture and kill all those found in the premises. A rapid reaction raid into the House might have saved at least some lives, if not all the lives. Shortly after getting information about the forcible entry of two terrorists into the Narriman House, a small police party reportedly reached the scene, but it did not apparently have either the numbers or the capability for immediate intervention. One had to wait for the arrival of the specially-trained National Security Guards (NSGs), which is a special intervention force. It arrived the next morning and took nearly 40 hours to enter the premises. By the time it could force its entry into the building it was late. All the six Jewish people had been killed by the terrorists after torturing them. Only an Indian maid managed to escape with a two-year-old Jewish child. While the Israeli authorities have praised the role of the Indian security forces in dealing with the situation and the co-operation extended by the Government of India, a note of regret over the delayed intervention was evident in some of their remarks.

While acknowledging the complexity of ending the attacks across sprawling Mumbai, Ehud Barak, the Israeli Defence Minister, told an Israeli TV channel on November 28: "I'm not sure it had to last three days, but that's what happened." Barak told Channel 1 Television that the bodies of two women and three men had been found at the religious-cum-cultural centre. The body of a third woman was found later in the building. Barak added that some of the bodies had been tied up, and that two women had been killed many hours before. "All in all, it was a difficult spectacle," he said.

The Defense Minister said that the roots of the attack were in India, but involved militants in Pakistan and Afghanistan. While he did not elaborate, his comments seemed to indicate that the Israeli authorities suspected that it must have been a joint operation of jihadis of India, Pakistan and Afghanistan and not just Pakistan as claimed by India.

One could discern notes of criticism in the comments of retired security experts and other private experts too. A former head of Israel's Mossad external intelligence agency, Danny Yatom, said the attacks revealed major failings in Indian intelligence as they "involved dozens of terrorists enjoying the support of numerous sympathizers." "It is vital that the Indian security services draw the necessary lessons," Yatom told a local radio station.

The head of Israel's counter-terrorism department, Colonel Nitzan Nurieli, said: "We have to acknowledge that in the Mumbai case our intelligence services did not have adequate advance knowledge; nor did the Indian security services." He urged Israeli tourists to avoid travel to northern India.

Ms Tzipi Livni, the Israeli Foreign Minister said: "There is no doubt, we know, that the targets the terrorists singled out were Jewish, Israeli targets and targets identified with the West, Americans and Britons. Our world is under attack, it doesn't matter whether it happens in India or somewhere else. There are Islamic extremists who don't accept our existence or Western values."

Israeli counter-terrorism experts compared the Mumbai strike to an attempted sea-borne terrorist strike in Tel Aviv in April 2003, when two British Muslims of Pakistani origin, were allegedly recruited by Al Qaeda, to land by sea in Tel Aviv, seize a large beachside hotel and the nearby US embassy, take hostages and shoot as many as possible. Recruited at London's radical Finsbury Park mosque (like Shoe-bomber Richard Reid) Asif Muhammed Hanif and Omar Khan Sharif were trained in Syria and the Gaza Strip.

After the Mombasa attack on Israeli tourists by Al Qaeda in November, 2002, in which 13 Israelis were killed, this was the second most devastating attack on Jewish people outside Israel since 9/11. Some Israeli analysts compared the deliberate attack on Jewish people in Mumbai to the attack on the Israeli athletes at the time of the Munich Olympics in 1972. It was even alleged that the terrorist attack on the Jewish people in Mumbai was handled as incompetently by the Indian counter-terrorism machinery as the attack on the Israelis in Munich was handled by the then West German counter-terrorism machinery. There were allegations of Indian arrogance — which was compared to the alleged West German arrogance — in reportedly declining to accept Israeli offers of assistance in terminating the terrorism situation in the Narriman House.

Foreign, including Israeli analysts, seemed to have difficulty in accepting the Indian version that only 10 terrorists were involved and that there was no local involvement. Their view was that an operation of this type could not have been carried out by just 10 terrorists and that too without local help. A widespread impression was that in their anxiety to focus on the LeT involvement, Indian investigators might be missing vital clues about an Al Qaeda hand which would be necessary to prevent a repeat of November 26.

While the modus operandi of terrorists coming stealthily by sea and taking the security forces by surprise had been seen in the past in Sri Lanka and Israel, a new MO seen for the first time in Mumbai was what some Israeli experts described as the human cluster bomb tactics. In a cluster bomb, a number of bombets separate from a mother bomb and spread in different directions killing or maiming people in their path.

Ten terrorists reached Mumbai, split into four groups and spread in different directions. Two terrorists went round the areas close to the sea front and killed people indiscriminately through hand-held weapons. One of them was killed and another captured — but not before they had killed at least about 70 innocent civilians.

A task of this group apparently was to keep the police preoccupied in hunting for them and to prevent it from going to the main scenes of attack, which had a strategic significance. These were the Taj Mahal Hotel, the Oberoi and Trident hotels, belonging to the same management and located side by side, and the Narriman House.

The delayed response of the NSG and the failure of the local authorities to keep the media out of the scenes of confrontation by imposing a curfew, if necessary, or, at least, by switching off all TV transmissions till the operation was over resulted in three consequences. Firstly, despite the outstanding bravery of the Police and NSG officers, the credibility of India's rapid response mechanism was damaged in the eyes of the Indian public and international opinion. Secondly, the TV transmissions even as the confrontation was going on enabled the terrorists to find out what was going on outside without the intervention forces being able to find out what was going on inside. The TV channels unwittingly provided an asymmetric operational advantage to the terrorists. Thirdly, the terrorists received a colossal supply of oxygen in the form of publicity, which could increase the flow of volunteers for more terrorist strikes in future.

It was evident the terrorist strike had three strategic objectives: firstly, to discredit the Indian political leadership and counter-terrorism apparatus. Secondly, to damage our tourist economy and to create nervousness in the minds of foreign investors about the security of life and property in India. Thirdly, to disrupt the strategic co-operation between India and Israel.

The investigation by the Mumbai Police, assisted by the Intelligence Bureau (IB) and the Research & Analysis Wing (R&AW), had a three-point focus: the role of the LeT and any others involved; the role of the ISI; and a reconstruction of the entire strike.

One got the impression that while the first two received adequate attention, the third did not receive the immediate attention it deserved. Without a satisfactory reconstruction, our ability to prevent a repetition of Mumbai — November 26 in other cities would be weak.

The Mumbai Police and the Maharashtra Government

continue to assert, on the basis of the interrogation of the arrested perpetrator that only 10 terrorists were involved. The operation involved detailed intelligence collection, reconnoitering the places to be attacked and the final planning and execution. It is difficult to accept that the same 10 persons performed all these tasks. There definitely must have been more people involved in the conspiracy on the ground in India, in addition to the Pakistan-based conspirators mentioned in the final investigation report of the police — at least performing peripheral roles such as intelligence collection and reconnoitering.

Jihadi terrorists indulge in acts of collective brutality and individualized brutality. The collective brutality is in the form of planting improvised explosive devices (IEDs) in public places, throwing hand-grenades into crowds, etc. There is no face-to-face brutalization. Individualized brutality is face-to-face brutalization of targeted individuals. We had in the past seen instances of individualized brutality in J&K, but not in Indian territory outside J&K. There were many reports from Mumbai of individualized face-to-face brutality against Indian and Israeli nationals and other Jews.

An organization called the Deccan Mujahideen (DM) was reported to have claimed responsibility in a message sent to the Indian media. Some reports said this message had originated from a computer in Pakistan. The word Deccan refers to South India and was widely used during the British rule. It is now rarely used in India, but in Pakistan it continues to be used widely. Many Pakistanis refer to the Indian Hyderabad as Hyderabad, Deccan, to distinguish it from Hyderabad in Sindh. After independence in 1947, the ruler of the state of Hyderabad, who was known as the Nizam of Hyderabad, and the ruler of the State of Junagadh in Gujarat, who was known as the Nawab of Junagadh, hesitated to join the Indian Union. Jawaharlal Nehru, the then Prime Minister, sent the Army into Hyderabad to merge it with India. Junagadh also joined India without the need for using the Army there. Many pro-Pakistan Muslims from Hyderabad fled to Karachi and settled down there. The LeT has long enjoyed some support from the descendents of some Muslims who migrated to Karachi from Hyderabad and Junagadh. It describes Hyderabad and Junagadh as Pakistani territory illegally occupied by India. One of its objectives is to liberate J&K, Hyderabad and Junagadh from what it describes as Hindu rule. It is possible that some of these Muslims originating from Hyderabad were constituted by the LeT into an organization called the Deccan Mujahideen and told to claim responsibility for the Mumbai terrorist strike. The ISI and the LeT are known to adopt this MO of asking someone else to claim responsibility in order to conceal their own involvement. During the Kargil conflict of 1999, the Pakistani Army shot down a plane of the Indian Air Force. The Hizbul Mujahideen (HM), an Indian terrorist organization whose leader Syed Salahuddin is based in Pakistan, claimed responsibility for the shooting. Subsequently, the R&AW intercepted a telephone conversation between Lt.Gen. Mohammad Aziz, the then Chief of the General Staff (CGS), and Musharraf, who was then in Beijing. In that tape, which was released by the Government to the media, Aziz clearly said that the Army shot down the Indian aircraft and asked the HM to claim responsibility. Musharraf replied: "Very good."

It is very difficult to carry out an operation of this nature by a group of Pakistanis without at least the logistic support of some Indian Muslims. India's home-grown jihadis fall into two groups. The first group consists of those who have joined the LeT and the HUJI and have been helping them. These are the fifth columnists in the Indian Muslim community. The second group consists of those calling themselves the Indian Mujahideen (IM), who maintain they have no links with the ISI or the Pakistani jihadi organizations. The IM was responsible for the serial explosions in many cities since November 2007. It also claimed responsibility for the Mumbai suburban train blasts of July, 2006. There was no evidence to show that the IM might have been involved in the 26/11 terrorist strike. The involvement of the group of fifth columnists is a strong likelihood. The Mumbai Police's conclusion was that only two Indian Muslims — Faheem Mohammad Ansari and Sabauddin Ahmed — were involved in collecting topographical information long before the terrorist strike. Vital information such as the stay of some Jewish people in the Narriman House and about the fact that the Taj Mahal Hotel had little security at the back entrance through which the terrorists reportedly entered did not appear to have come from these two Indian Muslims. This information could not have been collected through the Internet. How did the LeT get such operationally vital information? It could have got it only from some local accomplices or by a previous visit to Mumbai for local enquiries.

In a telephonic message to the British Broadcasting Corporation (BBC) in the second week of February, 2009, Mustafa Abu-al Yazid, who has been projected since 2007 as in charge of Al Qaeda operations in Afghanistan in liaison with the Neo Taliban of Mulla Mohammad Omar, warned India in the following words: "We send a short and succinct message to the Indian Government. The Mujahideen will never allow you to invade the Muslims and their lands in Pakistan. If you beguile yourselves into doing this, know well that you will pay a very heavy price, which you will regret much. We will call upon our whole Muslim nation, its Mujahideen and its martyrdom squads against you. We will strike your interests and your economic lifelines wherever they may be until you are demolished and bankrupt as America is being demolished and going bankrupt today. The Islamic nation which produced the audacious and heroic martyrs of Bombay, who struck you in the midst of your homes and humiliated you, is able to produce thousands more like them. You cannot be more powerful or have more ability than the Soviet Union which was destroyed on the rocks of the Afghanistan mountains nor Americans whose nose we rubbed in the dirt of Afghanistan, Iraq and Somalia." The authenticity of the message could not be established.

In one's anxiety to get as much information as possible from the captured terrorist, one did not seem to have paid attention to the important aspect of debriefing all the foreign survivors in the two hotels attacked as to what exactly happened. All of them, after their release, immediately went back to their respective countries .We do not have their version of what happened inside the hotels.

The inadequacies of our intelligence and investigating agencies and of the legal infrastructure against terrorism were known earlier. The startling new revelation was the inadequacies in our physical security apparatus, which made the terrorist strike possible and in our rapid response mechanism, which was brought out by the long time taken to terminate the terrorism situation.

Mumbai is our economic capital. The corporate headquarters of many leading — Indian and foreign — companies are located there. Many of our sensitive establishments, such as the Bombay High off-shore oil installations and some nuclear establishments are also located there. One would have, therefore, expected that our physical security infrastructure in Mumbai would have been the strongest. Instead it was found to have been very weak and was unable to deny success to the terrorists despite the availability of advance intelligence about the LeT's plans for a sea-borne act of terrorism. If it was so weak in Mumbai, one had reasons to be worried regarding the shape of the physical security infrastructure in other cities.

The terrorist strike and its sequel brought out the totally disjointed manner in which our entire counter-terrorism machinery — the intelligence agencies, the Armed Forces, particularly the Navy, the Police, the National Security Guards, the National Security Council Secretariat (NSG) and the Joint Intelligence Committee — were functioning without any synergy in thinking or action. While the poor reflexes of the Police in dealing with terrorism were known earlier and had been crying for attention for many years, the poor reflexes of the Navy — particularly on the West Coast, which is the most vulnerable to terrorist attacks by sea — were a matter of concern. After 9/11, we have been holding joint counter-terrorism exercises with many countries, including China. No such exercise seemed to have been held among the various agencies of our counter-terrorism community in order to test periodically their ability to act jointly in specific situations.

Our counter-terrorism strategy is a fits and starts strategy. In our preoccupation with handling the sequel to the Mumbai strike, we should not lose sight of the investigation into the serial blasts in Uttar Pradesh, Jaipur, Bangalore, Ahmedabad and Delhi, which involved home-grown jihadis. There is very little progress in identifying the command and control of the so-called Indian Mujahideen (IM) and in taking action to neutralize it. The threat posed by the home-grown jihadis has not diminished. On the contrary, it could increase further due to copy-cat effects of Mumbai.

IMPACT ON THE BUSINESS WORLD

India has been attacked by the jihadi terrorists — home-grown as well as of Pakistani origin — for many years. Despite this, the international business community with interests in India had confidence in the capability of the Indian counter-terrorism machinery to prevail over them and in their ability to protect the lives and property of foreign business executives working and living in India. In justification of their continuing confidence in the Indian counter-terrorism machinery, they remembered the successful record of India in dealing with the insurgency in the North-East, the Khalistani terrorism in Punjab, the Al Ummah terrorism in Tamil Nadu and even in controlling the jihadi terrorism in Jammu & Kashmir (J&K). That confidence was shaken at least temporarily after the Mumbai strike of November 26. This was seen in the advisories which were issued by private risk assessment consultancy groups to their business clients. The image of an India that can in the fight against terrorism gave way to an image of an India that probably can't. One more November 26 in any city with a large population of foreign businessmen — the nervousness can turn into panic.

In an article on the terrorist strike in Mumbai, the *Guardian* of the UK wrote: "Analysts are worried that the constant reminder of the attacks will heighten investors' concerns at a time when the Indian economy is slowing and foreign capital is being repatriated. 'This is the last thing India needs,' said businessman Sir Gulam

Noon. The British-based multimillionaire, who made his fortune in ready meals, escaped unhurt from the Taj Mahal after spending a frightening night holed up in his suite on the third floor. 'The attacks will temporarily have an impact. It's clearly not good for the economy at a time when the world is in a financial crisis.' That the Taj Mahal and Oberoi play host to the cream of the international business elite is clear given the high-profile executives caught up in the tragedy. Along with Noon, Unilever chief executive Patrick Cescau and his successor, Paul Polman, escaped the Taj Mahal. 'The security landscape has changed overnight,' said Jake Stratton of investment risk consultancy Control Risks. 'This will have a serious effect on how foreign companies perceive India as a business destination.'"

Terrorist attacks directed against economic and business targets have a tactical as well as a strategic impact, an economic as well as a psychological impact. The tactical impact is in respect of replaceable damages. The strategic impact has a long-term effect on the profitability of their business operations due to factors such as an increase in insurance premium for business transactions, an increase in their expenditure on physical security, and an increase in their tax liability due to a surge in Government spending on counter-terrorism for which the money has to come from the tax-payers. It has been estimated that the 9/11 terrorist strikes have resulted in a one-third increase in the expenditure on counter-terrorism in the US Defence Department alone. This does not include the expenditure of the Department of Homeland Security. The total US expenditure on counter-terrorism now reportedly amounts to US $ 500 billion per annum, which is 20 per cent of the total federal budget. This money has to come from the tax-payers.

The psychological impact arises from the nervousness of the business community. A businessman, who ventures abroad, looks for two things — profitability and security of life and property. If we are not able to assure the security of life and property, no amount of profitability will induce him to take the risk of operating from India.

Terrorists calculate that repeated and sustained successful terrorist strikes against capabilities would make the States more amenable to pressure and intimidation from them than successful terrorist strikes against human beings. Their calculations are not far wrong. In the case of terrorism against capabilities, even fears or rumors of a possible terrorist strike against them can have a negative effect on the economy.

Protection of capabilities against terrorist strikes has, therefore, become an important component of counter-terrorism. Protection of the capabilities of the State is the exclusive responsibility of the State for which it has a preventive intelligence capability and specially trained physical security agencies or forces.

Protection of the capabilities in the private sector is basically the responsibility of the physical security set-ups of the companies concerned, but the State too has an important responsibility for guiding them and helping them to improve their physical security set-ups through appropriate advice. There may be sensitive industries in the private sector, where the State's role extends beyond guidance and advice to actually buttressing the physical security set-up of the company through its (the Government's) own trained and armed personnel.

Effective physical security rests on a strong information base. The security set-ups of private companies and other establishments suffer from a major handicap in this regard. Their ability to collect intelligence is confined to the interior of the company or establishment. They will have no means of collecting intelligence about threats, which could arise from outside the company or establishment.

For this awareness of likely external threats they are dependent on the media, the police and the governmental intelligence agencies. The media reporting often tends to be sensational and over-dramatized. The reliability of their reports is often questionable. While open source information from the media is important for increasing awareness of likely threats, the ability to have it verified, analyzed and assessed is equally important. Otherwise, physical security set-ups will be groping in the dark.

Such verification, analysis and assessment have to come from the Police and the intelligence agencies and the results of this process have to be shared promptly with the companies or establishments, which are likely to face a threat, with appropriate suggestions for follow-up action. It should not be left to the security set-ups of private companies to take the initiative to contact the police and other counter-terrorism agencies to find out if there are any external threats to them — particularly after reading media reports in this regard.

The police and other counter-terrorism agencies should play a proactive role in creating and strengthening credible information awareness among the heads of the security set-ups of vulnerable private companies and their CEOs. This has to be constantly achieved through periodic interactions organized by the police in the form of brain-storming sessions, round-table discussions, etc. Such interactions at the initiative of the governmental agencies seem to be more sporadic than regular — often triggered only by an actual crisis than by the anticipation of a possible crisis.

Heads of the security set-ups of private companies should have easy access, when warranted, to senior officers of the police and other counter-terrorism agencies. One gets an impression that such access is often restricted to officers at the middle or lower levels, who do not have the required degree of professionalism and self-confidence to be able to interact meaningfully and satisfactorily with senior officers of the private sector.

The effective physical security of any establishment — sensitive or non-sensitive, private or public — depends on effective access control. Access control is ensured through means such as renewable identity cards for the permanent members of the staff; temporary identity cards to outsiders coming on legitimate work; numbered invitation cards to those invited to conferences, meetings, etc; restrictions on the entry of vehicles of outsiders into the campus; restricting the number of entry points and exits to the minimum unavoidable; identity checking at doors; checking for weapons and explosives through door-frame detectors; checking of vehicles for explosives; installation of closed circuit TV at the points of entry and exit and at sensitive points in the establishment; a central control room to monitor all happenings at the entry points and exits and inside the premises through the CCTV, etc. Better access control by the security staff is facilitated through the advance sharing of information with them about the outsiders, who are expected to visit the premises for meetings, conferences, seminars, etc.

These are the minimum measures necessary for any company or establishment, which is considered vulnerable to terrorist strikes. It is important for the Police to prepare and revise periodically lists of vulnerable companies/establishments in their jurisdiction and share their conclusions with the security set-ups concerned.

Similarly, it is important for each vulnerable company or establishment to prepare and revise periodically a list of vulnerable points/occasions, which would need the special attention of the security staff and brief the security staff on the follow-up action to be taken. It would also be necessary to discuss this list with the Police and seek their advice on the adequacy of the security measures, which the security set-up of the company or establishment proposes to take. The Police should not consider such consultations as unnecessary intrusions on their time. They should welcome such consultations or interactions as a necessary component of their counter-terrorism strategy.

IT companies and other establishments in South India often face work interruptions due to hoax telephone calls and e-mail and fax messages regarding possible terrorist strikes. A basic principle in physical security is, "treat every information, hoax call, etc as possibly correct unless and until it is proved to be false and take the necessary follow-up action. Never start on the presumption that the information is probably false or the message a hoax. This would be extremely inadvisable and even dangerous."

A well-prepared and frequently rehearsed crisis management drill is a very important part of the counter-terrorism strategy in any establishment — private or public. Effective physical security is the outcome of constant enhancements in the security personnel of professionalism, self-confidence, information awareness, threat and vulnerability perceptions and protective capability. Achieving these enhancements is primarily the responsibility of the security set-up of the establishment, but the Police has an important role in facilitating this. This is a responsibility, which they should not evade. Well-structured police security set-up interactions to enhance security in the private sector is the need of the hour.

Business resilience and business continuity management in terrorism-affected situations are two concepts increasingly figuring in discourses in the Western countries. They have also formed the subject of many studies by the business community and the counter-terrorism community — separately of each other as well as jointly. It is said that the best contribution that the business community can make to counter-terrorism is by staying in business despite terrorist strikes. They may not be able to do it alone. The Government has to help them by playing a proactive role.

New ideas and new institutions have come up in the West to promote partnership between the Government and the business community for ensuring their security and for keeping their resilence undamaged. One example is the Overseas Security Assistance Council established in 1985 by the US State Department to facilitate the exchange of security related information between the US Government and the American private sector operating abroad.

Another example is the creation of posts of Counter-Terrorism Security Advisers in important police stations in the UK after the London blasts of July, 2005. One of their tasks is to keep in touch with the business establishments in their jurisdiction and advise them on security-related matters. 243 posts of Counter-Terrorism Security Advisers have been created since July, 2005 and it has been reported that each important Police Station in London has at least two advisers attached to it. The London Police have established a program called "London First" in which the Police and the private sector co-operate closely to ensure better security in London. The principle underlying it is that it is the joint responsibility of everyone in London to ensure its security from terrorist attacks. Let us have our own Delhi First, Mumbai First, Chennai First, Kolkata First, Bangalore First and Hyderabad First partnerships to ensure that November 26 will not be repeated again.

Indian Army troops at the besieged Trident and Oberoi hotels on the night of November 26. *(Photograph: Uttam Ghosh/rediff.com)*

Mumbai police search the getaway Skoda used by Pakistani gunman Ajmal Amir Kasab and his accomplice Abu Ismail, soon after capturing Kasab at Chowpatty, November 26. *(Photograph: Uttam Ghosh/rediff.com)*

Foreign citizens, evacuated from the burning and besieged Taj Mahal Palace and Tower, outside the hotel, November 26. Many guests were still trapped inside the hotel at the time. *(Photograph: Uttam Ghosh/rediff.com)*

Morgue attendants and ambulance workers from the city's hospitals keep vigil outside the Trident and Oberoi hotels, November 26.
(Photograph: Uttam Ghosh/rediff.com)

The heritage wing of the Taj Mahal Palace and Tower aflame, November 26. The Mumbai Fire Brigade evacuated hotel guests trapped inside.
(Photograph: Uttam Ghosh/rediff.com)

Mumbai policemen confer outside the Taj Mahal Palace and Tower,
November 26. (*Photograph: Uttam Ghosh/rediff.com*)

Thousands and thousands of Mumbai citizens gathered near the Gateway of India, December 1, for a protest rally in the wake of 26/11. A newly re-opened Leopold Café is in the background. *(Photograph: Sanjay Sawant/rediff.com)*

Ajmal Amir Kasab's blood-spattered shoes were left on the road at Chowpatty, after the police captured him following a shoot-out and a physical scuffle, November 26. Next to the shoes lies a spent bullet.
(Photograph: Sanjay Sawant/rediff.com)

A relative waits anxiously outside the Trident hotel, Nariman Point, November 26, for the release of a family member trapped inside.
(Photograph: Sanjay Sawant/rediff.com)

Slain Mumbai Anti-Terrorism Squad chief Hemant Karkare's family at the Shivaji Park crematorium, November 29. *(Photograph: Sanjay Sawant/rediff.com)*

Farhang S Jehani, owner of the popular Leopold Café in south Mumbai, at his restaurant after it re-opened on December 2. Ten people were killed at the café and in the nearby street, by terrorists headed for the Taj Mahal Palace and Tower hotel. Jehani survived. *(Photograph: Dominic Xavier/rediff.com)*

A massive explosion, triggered by National Security Guard commandos, shattered the walls of the fourth floor of Nariman House, and made a huge gaping hole in the wall along the stairway, November 28. *(Photograph: Rajesh Karkera/rediff.com)*

Jubilant crowds gathered to cheer National Security Guard commandos after they
freed Nariman House of terrorists, November 28.
(Photograph: Rajesh Karkera/rediff.com)

A National Security Guard commando sprints towards the Taj Mahal Palace and
Tower hotel for a better position, November 28.
(Photograph: Sanjay Sawant/rediff.com)

Indian Army troops take position between the convoy of parked ambulances and fire engines outside the Taj Mahal Palace and Tower hotel, November 28. *(Photograph: Sanjay Sawant/rediff.com)*

A grenade lobbied by the terrorists at the Taj Mahal Palace and Tower explodes just outside the hotel scattering shrapnel, November 28. *(Photograph: Sanjay Sawant/rediff.com)*

Hundreds of journalists and cameramen from news organizations across the world camped for three days continuously outside the Taj Mahal Palace and Tower hotel. *(Photograph: Sanjay Sawant/rediff.com)*

The smashed Skoda terrorists Ajmal Amir Kasab and Abu Ismail stole to flee from Nariman Point. The police barricaded Marine Drive and captured Kasab and shot Ismail dead. *(Photograph: Uttam Ghosh/rediff.com)*

At Mumbai's Cama and Albless hospital a wreath marks the spot where one of the hospital's watchmen, Baban Ugre, was shot dead by Ajmal Amir Kasab and Abu Ismail, after the terrorists killed 52 people at the Chhatrapatti Shivaji Terminus nearby. *(Photograph: Reuben N V/rediff.com)*

The Taj Mahal Palace and Tower hotel smolders, November 27, as firefighters
battle the flames and commandos combat the terrorists.
(Photograph: Vaihayasi Pande Daniel/rediff.com)

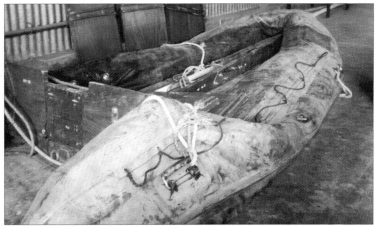

The rubber dinghy used by the 10 terrorists to land at Badhwar Park, Cuffe Parade, November 26, after disembarking from MS Kuber that brought them from Porbandar, Gujarat. *(Photograph: Vaihayasi Pande Daniel/rediff.com)*

An endless, hushed stakeout in the deserted streets of Colaba by the police, paramilitary troopers, army soldiers and commandos outside Nariman House is broken by the arrival of Major General R K Hooda, General Officer Commanding, Maharashtra, Goa and Gujarat area, in the middle of the night, November 27. *(Photograph: Vaihayasi Pande Daniel/rediff.com)*

MS Kuber, the trawler the 10 terrorists sailed on from Porbandar, Gujarat, to Mumbai, parked under police security at Chamar Godi, Carnac Bunder, central Mumbai. It is the brown, wood-paneled, fishing boat with a white flag in the centre. *(Photograph: Vaihayasi Pande Daniel/rediff.com)*

Two policemen, one in plain clothes, armed with guns and rifles stealthily edge closer towards the Trident hotel, November 27. *(Photograph: Satish Bodas/rediff.com)*

After setting off an enormous explosion, National Security Guard commandos take stock of the situation from their perch on the roof of Nariman House, November 28. The terrorists who besieged this building for three days were hiding in the floors below and were slain a few hours later. (*Photograph: Rajesh Karkera/rediff.com*)

PAKISTAN : THE SAME OLD STORY

The US pressured India into not retaliating against Pakistan after the attempted attack on the Indian Parliament by Pakistani terrorists on December 13, 2001, and promised that Pakistan would be made to dismantle the anti-Indian terrorist infrastructure in its territory. In response to the US pressure, India exercised moderation and did not exercise its right to retaliate. The promises made to India were never kept. The anti-Indian terrorist infrastructure in Pakistani territory continued to grow without the West taking any action against Pakistan.

The result: the savage attack of November 26–29, 2008. The US and the other Western countries conducted themselves in exactly the same way as they did in 2001 — expressions of outrage over the terrorist strike, pretense of solidarity with India, but at the same time ill-concealed attempts to protect Pakistan and its military-intelligence complex from the consequences of their continuing to sponsor terrorism against India in Indian territory.

Pakistan's behavior — whether it is ruled by elected political or military rulers — has not changed one iota since it started using terrorism against India in 1981. It would organize an act of terrorism and to pre-empt a possible Indian retaliation would project itself as the victim-State threatened by India and manipulate Western policy-makers into rationalizing its use of terrorism against India and pressuring India not to retaliate against Pakistan.

One thought and hoped that the West would act more firmly against Pakistan this time than it had done in the past because of the fact that the LeT terrorists, who attacked Mumbai, killed six Israelis and 19 other foreigners. These hopes were belied.

Instead of stepping up pressure on Pakistan to dismantle the LeT's terrorist infrastructure in Pakistani territory and arrest and hand over to India those involved in the orchestration of the terrorist strike in Mumbai, pressure was stepped up on India not to retaliate against Pakistan — not even politically. Instead of calling Pakistan to account for the outrage, attempts were made to mollify it by accepting the various conditions sought to be imposed by it, one of the conditions being that it would, if India produced evidence, prosecute the terrorists in its own courts and would not hand them over to India.

This was the fifth time Pakistan had defied international pressure to hand over criminal suspects for investigation and prosecution. The first was Omar Sheikh, one of the principal accused in the case relating to the kidnapping and murder of Daniel Pearl, the US journalist, at Karachi in January–February, 2002. It got him tried and sentenced to death by one of its courts. The hearing on his appeal has been adjourned by the anti-terrorism court over a hundred times. In the meanwhile, reports from Pakistan said that he had been given all the facilities such as mobile phones, etc that he asked for and that with these he was once again active from jail in guiding the pro-Al Qaeda jihadi terrorist organizations like the Jaish-e-Mohammad (JeM).

The second was Dawood Ibrahim, the Indian mafia leader, who is the principal accused in the case relating to the serial explosions in

Mumbai in March, 1993. He was designated by the US Department of Treasury as an international terrorist in October, 2003, because of his links with Al Qaeda and the LeT. Pakistan has avoided handing him over either to India or the US. He continues to live under an assumed name as a Pakistani national at Karachi. Even though sections of the Pakistani media have been periodically reporting about his presence and activities at Karachi, Pakistan continues to deny his presence in Pakistani territory.

The third was AQ Khan, the Pakistani nuclear scientist, found guilty of clandestinely transferring military nuclear technology to North Korea, Iran and Libya. Both the previous Government headed by Pervez Musharraf and the present Government headed by Asif Ali Zardari have consistently opposed demands that an international team of experts should be allowed to interrogate him outside Pakistan.

The fourth was Rashid Rauf, a British citizen of Mirpuri (Pakistan Occupied Kashmir) origin, who was arrested by the Pakistani authorities in August, 2006, on suspicion of his involvement in a plot discovered by the London Police to blow up a number of US-bound planes originating from British airports. He was the brother-in-law of Maulana Masood Azhar, the Amir of the Jaish-e-Mohammad (JeM). The Pakistani authorities repeatedly evaded action on a British request to hand him over so that they could interrogate him not only in connection with the alleged plot to blow up planes, but also in connection with the alleged murder of one of his relatives in Birmingham before he fled to Pakistan. He escaped from police custody under mysterious circumstances in December, 2007, and reportedly died in a missile strike by a US Predator (pilotless) plane on a suspected Al Qaeda- hide-out in North Waziristan on November 15, 2008.

The leaders of the LeT wanted by India in connection with the Mumbai attack constitute the fifth instance.

Pakistan's reluctance to hand over Omar Sheikh was due to the long history of contacts between him and the ISI and between him and Osama bin Laden. The Pakistani authorities wanted to prevent US interrogators from finding out about these contacts. Fears that Dawood Ibrahim's long history of contacts with the ISI, his contacts with Al Qaeda and the LeT and his role in helping AQ Khan in clandestinely transporting nuclear material to North Korea, Iran and Libya and North Korean missiles to Pakistan might come to the notice of the US during any interrogation have stood in the way of Pakistan handing him over either to India or the US. In the case of AQ Khan, fears that he might reveal the role of the political and military rulers in his clandestine proliferation activities are behind Pakistan's refusal to permit any independent interrogation of him. When the restrictions on his house arrest were relaxed after the elections of March 2008, he allegedly told some foreign journalists that Musharraf was totally in the picture about his nuclear and missile dealings with North Korea. The Government strongly denied these allegations and re-imposed the restrictions on him.

In the case of Rashid Rauf, it was alleged by many in Pakistan that he was aware of the contacts of the JeM with the ISI and of the identities of the elements in Pakistan which trained the suicide bombers, who carried out the London blasts of July 2005. The

LeT's close links with the ISI on the one side and with Al Qaeda on the other were believed to be behind the refusal to hand over the masterminds behind the Mumbai attack to the Indian authorities. If the US, through independent sources, collected more irrefutable evidence and maintained the pressure on Pakistan, the most Pakistan might do is to hold a proforma trial against the LeT operatives, get them jailed and allow them to guide the LeT activities from jail in the same manner as Omar Sheikh has been guiding the activities of the JeM from jail.

If the US is really concerned over the refusal of Pakistan to act against the LeT's terrorist infrastructure and operatives, it could declare Pakistan as a state-sponsor of terrorism and stop all military and economic assistance to it. However, it is unlikely to take this step due to fears that this might affect even the limited co-operation which Pakistan has been extending to the US in targeting Al Qaeda and Taliban sanctuaries.

India has failed to convince large sections of the international community that the ISI had orchestrated the 26/11 Mumbai terrorist strike. The experts of the various countries whose nationals died at the hands of the terrorists are convinced on the basis of their own substantial independent technical intelligence that the terrorist attack was carried out by Pakistani nationals belonging to the LeT, who came to Mumbai by boat from Karachi for carrying out the strike. They are also convinced on the basis of the voluminous evidence in their archives about the privileged relationship between the ISI and the LeT. But they claim not to have seen any conclusive evidence so far to show that the ISI had orchestrated the attack. A question, which they often posed during interactions in non-governmental discussions, was whether the terrorists would have killed nationals of the US, the UK, France, Italy, Germany, Canada and Australia if they had been deputed by the ISI to indulge in the carnage.

Some of these experts were earlier convinced of the ISI hand behind the attack on the Indian Embassy in Kabul in the first week of July, 2008, when Lt.Gen. Nadeem Taj was the ISI Director-General. They were prepared to allow for the possibility that Lt Gen Taj, before he was removed from the ISI on September 30, 2008, allegedly under US pressure by Gen Pervez Ashfaq Kayani, Pakistan's Chief of the Army Staff (COAS), might have also planned the Mumbai attack by the LeT and got its cadres chosen for the attack trained. In this connection, it is significant that Ajmal Kasab, the lone Pakistani survivor now facing trial, had reportedly stated during his interrogation that the attack was planned for September 26, but was postponed. These experts pointed out that Taj was still the DG of the ISI on September 26, 2008.

The Americans had allegedly got Taj removed because of their conviction that his was the brain behind the Kabul attack and that Taj, who has a reputation of being rabidly anti-Indian and anti-US, had leaked out some information shared by the Americans with him to the Taliban. While thus some American experts had an open mind on the possibility of the involvement of Taj in the Mumbai carnage, they tended to give the benefit of doubt to Lt Gen Ahmed Shuja Pasha, who has been the DG of the ISI since September 30, 2008. He enjoyed a good reputation in the West as a balanced person, who would not indulge in this type of operation, particularly when it was partly directed against Western nationals and Jewish civilians.

Apart from the way the attack was planned and executed, the most significant aspect of the attack was the targeting of foreign nationals — particularly the cream of the foreign business community who frequent these hotels. It was because of this that the technical intelligence agencies of the Western countries diverted all their capabilities to cover the conversations between the terrorists and their handlers in Pakistan. It was said in well-informed counter-terrorism circles that the US moved one of its communication satellites over Mumbai during the 60 hours that the drama lasted in order to cover these conversations.

After the drama was over and the National Security Guards (NSGs) had rescued the surviving hostages, the Western countries had all their surviving nationals quietly flown to Europe where they were thoroughly debriefed by special teams from their intelligence agencies. It is said that the French even sent a special plane for evacuating the French and other Western survivors from Mumbai to Paris. Western experts were surprised that neither the Mumbai Police nor the central intelligence agencies showed interest in detaining the surviving foreign hostages in India in order to debrief them thoroughly. If they had done so, the details collected by them would have formed an important part of the dossier prepared by the Ministry of Home Affairs against Pakistan and disseminated to foreign Governments. It is learnt that such details, which could have been obtained by debriefing the foreign survivors, hardly figured in the dossier.

According to foreign experts, the Mumbai Police and the central intelligence agencies were so excited by the capture alive of one of the Pakistani perpetrators that they seemed to have devoted all their attention to interrogating him and getting as many details as possible, which could help them to fix Pakistan. They complain that other important aspects which might have helped them in reconstructing the terrorist attack, drawing the right lessons from it and preventing a repetition of similar attacks in future did not receive much attention.

Despite what has been stated above, it must be admitted that the American pressure on Pakistan was a little more than in the past because of two reasons. First, because of the anger in Israel and the Jewish Diaspora in the West over the brutal massacre of six Israeli nationals — two of them with dual US nationality — and a Jewish person from Mexico. Second, because of the concerns of Western businessmen, with business interests in India, over the security of their life and property in India.

Under this pressure, Pakistan ostensibly acted against the JUD, through measures such as placing its Amir Pro. Hafeez Mohammad Sayeed under house arrest, arresting some cadres at senior, middle and junior levels, freezing the bank accounts of the organization, etc. Interestingly, it attributed its actions to the decision of the anti-terrorism committee of the UN Security Council to designate the JUD as a terrorist organization and blacklist four of its top leaders including Prof Sayeed. It sought to avoid adding to the anti-Government anger in the pro-jihadi sections of its population by creating an impression that its actions were dictated by the decision of the UN Anti-Terrorism Committee, which the Government was bound to obey, and not by US pressure.

Since the terrorist attack lasted 60 hours and the lives of the nationals of many countries were in danger, the intelligence agencies of India, Israel, the US and the UK — and possibly of other countries too — were monitoring through technical means the conversations of the terrorists holed up in the two hotels and in the Jewish centre with each other and with their controllers in Pakistan. Thus, a substantial volume of independent technical intelligence exists — collected by the intelligence agencies of these countries independently of each other.

On the basis of the evidence gathered by the Indian investigators and shared by the intelligence agencies of other countries with India, the Government of India demanded three things from Pakistan: firstly, the arrest and handing over to India for interrogation and prosecution of the Pakistan-based ring leaders of the conspiracy as named by Ajmal Amir Kasab, the only surviving perpetrator, who was caught by the Mumbai police; secondly, the arrest and handing over to India of 20 other accused in terrorism related cases pending before Indian courts who have been given shelter in Pakistan; and thirdly, the dismantling of the Pakistan-based terrorist infrastructure of the LeT.

As other Pakistani Governments had done in the past, the present Government headed by President Asif Ali Zardari too has refused to extend mutual legal assistance to India as required by the conventions followed by the Interpol and by the UN Resolution No.1373 adopted unanimously by the UN General Assembly after the 9/11 terrorist strikes in the US. It first even denied that the terrorist captured by the Mumbai Police is a Pakistani national despite Kasab's father identifying him as his son in an interview to the *Dawn*, the prestigious daily of Karachi. Under pressure from the US, it reluctantly admitted that he is a Pakistani national, but continued to question the credibility of the evidence collected by India. It made clear that there was no question of handing over any Pakistani national to India for trial.

Since Pakistan became independent in 1947, it has never handed over to India any Muslim — Pakistani or Indian — who had committed an offence in Indian territory — whether the offence is terrorism or theft or robbery or rape or child sex or narcotics smuggling or any other. The attitude of non-cooperation adopted by the present Government should not, therefore, be a matter of surprise. The international community should not allow Pakistan to get away with its brazen defiance of all international conventions relating to action against terrorists. If it manages to do so due to the reluctance of the international community to act against Pakistan, this won't bode well for the success of the war against terrorism.

India has to use three yard-sticks to decide on the genuiness and adequacy of any Pakistani co-operation. These are:

- Does its co-operation help in bringing to justice the operatives of the LeT in Pakistan and any others, who were involved in the planning and execution of the terrorist strike?

- Does its co-operation help in a better reconstruction and understanding of the terrorist strike in order to find out answers to some important questions such as why the terrorists targeted Israeli and other foreign nationals, for example? The answers to such questions will be available only with the master-minds of the LeT in Pakistan. Ajmal Amir Kasab, the surviving Pakistani perpetrator, now in the custody of the Mumbai Police, may not be privy to the objectives of the LeT.

- Does the Pakistani co-operation help India in preventing any more terrorist strike mounted from Pakistani territory — by the LeT, the other anti-India terrorist organizations and Al Qaeda by eradicating their terrorist infrastructure in Pakistani territory and destroying their capabilities?

There was some forward movement with regard to the first question on February 12, 2009, when Rehman Malik, Pakistan's Minister for Internal Security, who is known to be closer to President Asif Ali Zardari than to Prime Minister Yousef Raza Gilani,, handed over to the Indian High Commissioner in Islamabad the salient points of the Pakistani investigation and action taken till then with a list of 30 questions for India to answer to enable them to take the investigation further. These salient points were revealed by him to the media at a special press conference held the same day.

A careful study of the Pakistani media reports showed that Pakistan seemed to be more forthcoming than it was since 26/11 and was keen to demonstrate to the international community that in investigating the case "Pakistan means business" as Malik repeatedly emphasized. There was a seeming shift from a position of total denial of the involvement of anyone in Pakistani territory to a partial acceptance of the conclusion of Indian and Western investigators that the conspiracy for the terrorist attack originated in Pakistani territory and that the key answers to many questions which arose during the investigation were to be found in Pakistan, which only Pakistani investigators can do.

At the same time, there was an undisguised attempt by Malik to project the conspiracy as trans-national and not uni-national only in Pakistan. He repeatedly said that only a part of the conspiracy took place in Pakistani territory. To underline the trans-national dimensions of the conspiracy he referred to the role played by some members of the Pakistani Diaspora in Spain and Italy and to Pakistan's suspicion of a role by some elements in India as seen, according to him, from the fact that the perpetrators had used SIM cards procured in India.

Pakistan's attempt was to project the conspiracy as mounted by non-State elements of which the Pakistani intelligence agencies had no inkling till after the attack. There was a reluctance on the part of Indian analysts to accept that all the recruitment, planning and training could have been carried out by the LeT in Pakistani territory without the Pakistani intelligence agencies becoming aware of it. Malik seemed to have prepared the ground for meeting this argument if and when it acquired force by pointing out that if the intelligence agencies of India, Italy and Spain had missed noticing the preparations being made in their territory, how can one blame the Pakistani agencies for similarly missing them.

There were two significant points in the press briefing of Malik. The first was the absence of any reference to Indian allegations that a group of 32 potential perpetrators was trained by the LeT initially in Pakistan-Occupied Kashmir (PoK) and subsequently in Karachi before 10 of them were finally selected and sent to Mumbai by sea. The second was his repeated use of the word "alleged" while referring to the role of the LeT operatives, who had been detained and against whom investigations had been launched in pursuance of the two First Information Reports (FIRs) registered by the Federal Investigation Agency (FIA). He did not use the word "alleged" while referring to those whose involvement Pakistan claimed to have unearthed through its own investigation. This would indicate a possible attempt by them to show their investigation against some LeT operatives as warranted by the Indian "allegations" against them and not by any evidence so far uncovered by the FIA. Thus, while registering two FIRs against the LeT operatives named by India, they kept open the possibility of giving a clean chit to the LeT after the international pressure and interest subsided and releasing the LeT operatives on the ground that the investigation did not bring out any credible evidence against them.

This was exactly the same modus operandi (MO) which the Pakistanis had followed after the thwarted attack by a group of terrorists belonging to the LeT and the Jaish-e-Mohammad (JeM) on the Parliament House in New Delhi in December, 2001. Musharraf banned these organizations on January 15, 2002, arrested their leaders and ordered an enquiry into their activities. A few months later, they were quietly released and the enquiries discontinued.

While we were right in welcoming the changed Pakistani stance — even if it be only a change in tactics — as seen on February 12, 2009, we should avoid nursing illusions that the seeming change in the Pakistani stance marked a watershed in Pakistani attitude to anti-India terrorism. We have to wait and see whether Pakistan really means business this time, or is it merely pretending to co-operate while not sincerely co-operating as it has always done in the past — whether against anti-India terrorism or against the Neo Taliban of Afghanistan or against Al Qaeda.

Pakistan's new stance of seeming co-operation in the investigation of the Mumbai attack did not respond to the remaining two questions posed above. There are no indications at all that it is having second thoughts about the wisdom or inadvisability of continuing to use terrorism as a strategic weapon against India and that it might now act against the anti-India terrorist infrastructure in its territory and the role of the ISI in keeping this terrorism sustained. Threats of new terrorist attacks against Indian and foreign targets in Indian territory mounted from Pakistan remain as high as before.

Subsequent developments relating to the house arrest of Sayeed, the Amir of the JUD, justified India's suspicions regarding the sincerity of Pakistani assurances of co-operation in the investigation of the Mumbai attack. After the Mumbai attack, the Government of Pakistan took two actions. It ordered the arrest of five members of the LeT against whom specific evidence of their involvement had been produced by the Government of India. It was reported that the USA's Federal Bureau of Investigation (FBI) had also collected independent evidence against them. A case against them was registered for investigation and prosecution and their judicial remand was being extended from time to time by an Anti-terrorism court of Islamabad.

The second action was the placing under house arrest of Prof Sayeed, Col. (retd) Nazir Ahmed and some others not on the ground of their involvement in the Mumbai attack, but on the ground that they belonged to an organization, which had been designated by the anti-terrorism sanctions committee of the UN Security Council as a terrorist organization. While placing them under house arrest, the Government did not officially ban their organization as a terrorist set-up.

The Review Board set up by the Government to review the legality of the house arrests had upheld the Government decision. However, Prof Sayeed and Nazir Ahmed had challenged their house arrest as illegal before the Lahore High Court. Their lawyer appealed to the court to set aside their house arrest on two grounds. The first was that they were not supplied with the grounds of their house arrest as required under the law within the time-limit laid down. This vitiated the procedure followed, they claimed. The second ground was that the Government had passed its order of house arrest purely on the basis of the resolution of the UN Sanctions Committee, without any independent evidence of its own necessitating their house arrest.

In response to these arguments, the Government contended that it had independent evidence, including evidence of the LeT's links with Al Qaeda, and showed the evidence privately to the Bench without sharing it with the lawyers to Sayeed and his associate. The lawyers held this also as illegal since their clients had been deprived of their right to know all the grounds for their house arrest including the evidence on which they were based.

After considering these arguments, a three-member bench of the Lahore High Court held illegal on June 2, 2009, the house arrest of Prof Sayeed and his associate Col.(retd) Nazir Ahmed and ordered their release.

The final order explaining the release issued by the Bench on June 6, 2009, made the following observations: "The Government's decision to detain the Dawa leaders was not based on solid evidence and the material provided by the Government against them was incorrect and even prepared after their detention. The Government had no evidence that Sayeed and Nazir had any links with Al Qaeda or were involved in anti-state activities, except the 'bald allegations' leveled by the Indian lobby that they were involved in the Mumbai attacks. The material against the petitioners was mostly based on intelligence reports, which had been obtained after four months of their detention. Moreover, these reports were found to be incorrect as nothing apprehended in the reports actually took place. Several intelligence reports were obtained during the period when the petition was pending, apparently to cover the lacunae, but there was no solid evidence or source to supplement the reports. About the Dawa leaders' involvement in the Mumbai attacks, not a single document had been brought on the record that Dawa or the petitioners were involved in the said incident. There was no evidence that Dawa had links with Al Qaeda. The security laws and anti-terrorism laws of Pakistan were silent on Al Qaeda being a terrorist organization. Even after the perusal of these documents we do not find any material declaring that the detention was necessary for the security of the petitioners and there was no evidence that the petitioners had any links with Al Qaeda or any terrorist movement."

Thus, according to the court, no evidence was produced before it linking the JUD and its Amir with the 26/11 attacks. It has not only given a clean chit to the Amir, but also to his organization, namely, the LeT and held that there was no evidence of their being linked to Al Qaeda or any other terrorist movement. The Government has appealed against this judgment to the Supreme Court. If it concurs with the observations of the Lahore High Court, the criminal case filed separately against five members of the LeT for their involvement in 26/11 might also ultimately fail. From the way the case was handled from the beginning, it was evident that the Government, while acting against those LeT operatives whose involvement in the Mumbai attack was not deniable, wanted to protect Prof Sayeed, his organization and their terrorist infrastructure in Pakistani territory. The whole case was handled in such a manner as to make their release by the court inevitable and to weaken the case against the others facing prosecution before an anti-terrorism court.

The JUD, which played an active role in the humanitarian relief and rehabilitation operations in the PoK after the earthquake of October, 2005, is playing a similar role now in organizing relief for the internally-displaced Pashtuns from the Swat Valley of the North-West Frontier Province (NWFP) who have been forced to leave their villages in the Valley due to the counter-insurgency operations mounted by the Pakistan Army against the Pakistani Taliban. For this purpose, it has assumed a new identity as the Insaniyat (Humanity) Foundation. The Pakistani media has reported that this Foundation is nothing but the JUD and the LeT, but the Government has not taken any action against it.

Naivete has been the defining characteristic of the US policy towards Pakistan. One need not be surprised by this. Despite their close relations with Pakistan — particularly with its military-intelligence establishment — for over 50 years, Americans — whether in the Government or in private think tanks — do not understand Pakistan even though they think they do. We are the next door neighbours of Pakistan. We have had four military conflicts with Pakistan since 1947. We have been the victims of Pakistan-sponsored and Pakistan-aided terrorism since 1981. Despite this, we tend to be as naive as the Americans.

This became evident from the unwarranted euphoric reaction in policy-making and think-tank circles in New Delhi to remarks made by Zardari to a group of civil servants in Islamabad on July 7, 2009. According to the correspondent of the *Times of India* (July 9, 2009), Zardari reportedly said: "Militants and extremists were deliberately created and nurtured as a policy to achieve short-term tactical objectives. Let us be truthful and make a candid admission of the reality — the terrorists of today were the heroes of yesteryear until 9/11 and they began to haunt us as well".

His remarks were hailed in New Delhi as indicating a refreshing realization and admission by Zardari. But was he referring to the anti-India terrorist groups like the LeT? Not at all. From a careful reading of his remarks, it is evident he was referring to the Taliban, which has been spreading death and destruction in Pakistan. This was also evident from an editorial written by the *Daily Times* of Lahore on July 9, 2009. It said: "President Asif Ali Zardari, addressing the bureaucrats in Islamabad on Tuesday, made some 'candid admissions' that the Taliban policy of Pakistan in the past was wrong: 'the terrorists of today are the heroes of yesteryear'."

Thus, when Zardari talked of the heroes of yesterday becoming the terrorists of today, he was talking of the Taliban and not the LeT. At least, Musharraf spoke of the LeT as a suspected terrorist organization for some months in 2002. Zardari has never referred to the JUD or the LeT as a terrorist organization. He has not formally banned the JUD. He has not prevented the JUD from operating in the camps for internally-displaced Pashtuns under the name of the Insaniyat Foundation.

While refraining from criticizing the inaction of the Pakistani authorities in the cases relating to the LeT operatives and office-bearers involved in the Mumbai attack, the US kept its focus on the LeT in an attempt to reassure India that its non-criticism of Pakistan did not mean letting the LeT get away with its acts of terrorism against India. In a press note issued on July 1, 2009, the US Department of Treasury gave the personal particulars of four persons — a Pashtun born in Afghanistan, two Punjabis and a fourth person of unclear ethnicity originating from Karachi — associated with the LeT, who were designated by the Department under Executive Order 13224 as "providing direct support to Al Qaeda and the LeT and as facilitating terrorist attacks, including the July 2006 train bombing in Mumbai."

The four persons so designated by the Treasury Department were:

A. FAZEEL-A-TUL SHAYKH ABU MOHAMMED AMEEN

AL-PESHAWARI, born in the Konar Province of Afghanistan and living in Peshawar.

B. ARIF QASMANI, a Pakistani national from Karachi.

C. MOHAMMED YAHYA MUJAHID, a Pakistani national from Lahore.

D. NASIR JAVAID, a Pakistani national from Gujranwala, Punjab, living in Manshera, NWFP.

The Treasury Department's notification did not specifically refer to Fazeel-A-Tul Shaykh Abu Mohammed Ameen Al-Peshawari (Ameen al-Peshawari) as an associate or an office-bearer of the LeT. However, it said of him as follows: "He was providing assistance, including funding and recruits, to Al Qaeda network. He has also provided funding and other resources to the Taliban, including explosive vests and other resources and actively facilitated the activities of anti-Coalition militants operating in Afghanistan by raising money in support of terrorist activities. In addition, he had begun a campaign to support militants in Pakistan. As of 2007, Ameen al-Peshawari was responsible for recruiting fighters and suicide bombers and for the acquisition of funds and equipment for militants in Afghanistan. Ameen al-Peshawari has also provided monetary compensation to families of fighters killed in Afghanistan and has been involved in anti-Coalition militia recruiting activities." All the activities of Abu Mohammed al-Peshawari referred to in the notification related to Afghanistan.

However, Arif Qasmani of Karachi was specifically named by

the notification as involved in the Mumbai suburban train blasts of July, 2006, and in the Samjotha Express blast of February, 2007. It said of him as follows: "Arif Qasmani is the chief coordinator for Lashkar-e Tayyiba's (LeT) dealings with outside organizations and has provided significant support for LeT terrorist operations. Qasmani has worked with the LeT to facilitate terrorist attacks, including the July 2006 train bombing in Mumbai, India, and the February 2007 Samjotha Express bombing in Panipat, India. Qasmani conducted fundraising activities on behalf of the LeT in 2005 and utilized money that he received from Dawood Ibrahim, an Indian crime figure and terrorist supporter, to facilitate the July 2006 train bombing in Mumbai, India. Since 2001, Arif Qasmani has also provided financial and other support and services to Al Qaeda, including facilitating the movement of al Qaida leaders and personnel in and out of Afghanistan, the return of foreign fighters to their respective countries, and the provision of supplies and weapons. In return for Qasmani's support, Al Qaeda provided Qasmani with operatives to support the July 2006 train bombing in Mumbai, India, and the February 2007 Samjotha Express bombing in Panipat, India. In 2005, Qasmani provided Taliban leaders with a safe haven and a means to smuggle personnel, equipment, and weapons into Afghanistan."

From the notification, three significant points about Qasmani emerged: First, he received money from Dawood Ibrahim for the July 2006 bombings in Mumbai; second, he provided financial and logistics support to Al Qaeda and its leaders; and third, he provided safe haven to the leaders of the Afghan Taliban.

According to the notification, "Mohammed Yahya Mujahid is the head of the LeT media department and has served as an LeT media spokesman since at least mid-2001. In that capacity, Mujahid has issued statements to the press on behalf of the LeT on numerous occasions, including after the December 2001 LeT attacks on the Indian Parliament, and following the November 2008 attacks in Mumbai, India. Mujahid's statements on behalf of the LeT have been reported by international news sources such as BBC News, the *New York Times*, the *International Herald Tribune*, and *Asia Times Online*. As of late 2007, Mujahid was influential among the LeT central leadership."

The notification said that "Nasir Javaid is an LeT official involved in LeT operations and has served as an LeT commander in Pakistan. From 2001 to at least 2008, Nasir Javaid was also involved in LeT military training. In mid-2001, Javaid assumed command of an LeT training center in Pakistan."

The notification did not specify whether the evidence against the four designated individuals cited in it was collected by the US intelligence or whether some of it came from India too. Earlier on June 29, 2009, the Department of Public Information of the UN Security Council had announced as follows: "The Al Qaida and Taliban Sanctions Committee approved the addition of three entries to its Consolidated List of individuals and entities subject to the assets freeze, travel ban and arms embargo set out in paragraph 1 of Security Council resolution 1822 (2008) adopted under Chapter VII of the Charter of the United Nations." The three names added by the UN Committee to its list were those of Abu Mohammad Ameen al-

Peshawari, Arif Qasmani and Mohammad Yahya Mujahid. The name of Nasir Javaid did not figure in the list issued by the UN Committee possibly because there was no evidence of his involvement with Al Qaeda and/or the Afghan Taliban. The evidence against the three persons cited in the notification of the UN Committee was the same as subsequently cited by the US Treasury Department.

The UN Committee notification had one additional detail which was not there in the Treasury Department notification — namely, all the three persons were in custody as of June, 2009. While it did not mention where they were in custody, it must have been in Pakistan. It also did not say when they were arrested.

However, in a report on the Mumbai terrorist attack of November, 2008, carried by *Asia Times Online* on December 2, 2008, Syed Saleem Shahzad, its Special Correspondent in Pakistan, had indicated that Arif Qasmani, whom he described as a millionaire businessman of Karachi, was already in detention in Pakistan because of the ISI's anger over the double role allegedly played by him — namely, assisting the ISI in its operations in India through the LeT and at the same time assisting the Pakistani Taliban in its operations against the Pakistan Army.

Shahzad reported as follows: "The most important asset of the ISI, the Laskhar-e-Taiba (LeT), was split after 9/11. Several of its top-ranking commanders and office bearers joined hands with al-Qaeda militants. A millionaire Karachi-based businessman, Arif Qasmani, who was a major donor for ISI-sponsored LeT operations in India, was arrested for playing a double game — he was accused of working with the ISI while also sending money to Pakistan's South

Waziristan tribal area for the purchase of arms and ammunition for Al Qaeda militants."

Shahzad did not mention when Qasmani was arrested, but from the wording of his article it appeared that he must have been arrested before the 26/11 Mumbai strike. Earlier, the *Dawn* of Karachi had reported on December 29, 2005, as follows: "The Sindh High Court asked the federal interior secretary on Wednesday to file, within 10 days, a rejoinder to a petition alleging that a man was being detained by a federal law enforcement agency unlawfully. Petitioner Javeria Arif submitted through Advocate Nihal Hashmi that her husband, Arif Qasmani, was picked up by law enforcement personnel from his KDA Scheme residence on November 29 for his suspected links with Al Qaeda and the Taliban. No case was registered against him, nor was he produced before a magistrate for remand. The police were informed but was of no help to her. An additional advocate-general informed a division bench, comprising Justices Mushir Alam and Athar Saeed, that the provincial government had nothing to do with the matter but he required more time to make a formal statement on behalf of the police. Adjourning further hearing to January 19, the bench expressed its concern that, judging by the number of petitions being filed in this behalf, the incidence of 'disappearance' of people was on the increase. It observed that the government agencies were legally obliged to protect the life and liberty of citizens and they should act in accordance with the law."

On December 1, 2005, Shahzad reported to the Italian news agency AKI (Adnkronos International) as follows: "Arif Qasmani is a veteran jihadi, having fought against the Russian invasion of

Afghanistan in the 1980s, and been associated with the armed struggle in Indian-held Kashmir. He was picked up by Pakistani security forces last October but released a few days later. Now Qasmani is once again missing. According to his family, he was in Karachi and departed for Lahore two days ago but since he left home his whereabouts are unknown." Around the same time, he reported to Asia *Times Online* as follows: "Arif Qasmani was a part of a high-level November 14 meeting in Islamabad held to initiate a process for peace between the Afghan resistance and coalition forces led by the US."

The same day, Amir Mir, the well-known Pakistani journalist, who writes for sections of the Pakistani media and some of whose articles are also carried by sections of the Indian media, reported as follows: "One of the four Pakistanis who reportedly held a clandestine meeting with the visiting American Undersecretary of State for Public Affairs, Karen Hughes and other senior US State Department officials at Serena Hotel in Islamabad on November 14, 2005, to broker a deal between the Taliban and the United States is believed to have been kidnapped by the Pakistani intelligence agencies."

He added: "Previously linked with the now defunct Lashkar-e-Toiba, a militant outfit active in the Indian-administered Kashmir, Arif Qasmani is considered close to Javed Ibrahim Paracha, a former member of the National Assembly from Kohat district of the NWFP. Paracha, who is also the chairman of the World Prisoners' Relief Forum, claimed on November 17, 2005, that he was requested by the Americans during their Islamabad meeting to serve as a bridge between Washington, the Taliban and their Arab comrades for the purpose of 'reconciliation'. According to Paracha, Arif Qasmani has been picked up by the Pakistani intelligence agencies without any justification. 'Qasmani went missing on Tuesday after he had left Karachi for Lahore by plane which was supposed to take off at 8 in the morning. His wife has informed me that Qasmani has not yet reached Lahore where he was supposed to hold a business meeting. I understand that he has been arrested by the sensitive agencies. He was earlier detained in August 2005. His family members now fear for his life', Paracha said.

He further reported: "Paracha, who is also Chairman, International Rabita Jehad Council, said those who met the Americans on November 14 and discussed the possibility of negotiating with the Afghan resistance leaders included (besides him) Arif Qasmani, Khalid Khawaja and Shah Abdul Aziz of MMA (Muttahida Majlis-e-Amal, a religious coalition then in power in the NWFP) from Karak district in NWFP. 'There is every possibility that Qasmani has been detained for investigations in connection with the November 14 meeting', Paracha added. Khalid Khawaja, a former officer with the Inter-Services Intelligence (ISI) said, 'I have just met Arif Qasmani's wife in Karachi. She is much disturbed. She is shocked and believes that Qasmani has been kidnapped by the agencies who had previously detained him in August this year'. Khawaja said the family of the kidnapped businessman is seriously considering approaching the court of law for his recovery. 'I appeal to the government to inform his family members about his exact whereabouts. The government should ensure that Qasmani is recovered as early as possible', he added."

Thus, during his career, Arif Qasmani had helped the LeT, the ISI, the TTP and the US State Department. He had helped the LeT in its operations in India. He had helped the ISI by acting as its cut-out with the LeT in order to maintain the deniability of the ISI's use of the LeT against India. He had helped the Pakistani Taliban (TTP) in its operations against the Pakistan Army and the ISI. He had helped the US State Department by acting as an intermediary between it and the so-called good Taliban. He was also acting as the cut-out of Dawood Ibrahim for funding terrorist attacks in India and of Al Qaeda for using Pakistani jihadi cells in India for its operations. He was also associated with Khalid Khawaja, a retired officer of the Pakistan Air Force who had served in the ISI. Khawaja's name first cropped up during the investigation into the kidnapping and murder of Daniel Pearl, the journalist of the *Wall Street Journal*, at Karachi in January–February, 2002. Information regarding his role in the Pearl's case had alleged that it was he who had told the kidnappers that Pearl was Jewish.

It is surprising that a man with such a controversial background should be moving in and out of informal custody in Pakistan since August 2005 and at the same time assisting the LeT, Al Qaeda and the Taliban in their terrorist strikes, including the Mumbai attack of July, 2006, and the blast of February, 2007, in the Samjotha Express without ever being prosecuted under Pakistan's Anti-Terrorism Act. The State Department had known about him at least since 2005, if not earlier. Why has it acted against him only in June, 2009?

Why such lack of promptness in acting against the LeT? Even though the US and the European nations are increasingly concerned over the links of the LeT with Al Qaeda, its capability for acts of terrorism, which is second only to that of Al Qaeda and the presence of its sleeper cells among the Pakistani-origin Diaspora in many countries, they still look upon it as a looming and not an imminent threat to their nationals and interests. For them, the imminent threat is from Al Qaeda and the Taliban. Their present efforts are focused on making Pakistan act against the imminent threats while exercising only proforma pressure — to reassure India of their solidarity — on Pakistan to act against the LeT. As a result, Pakistan's inaction against the LeT tends to be overlooked by the West so long as it is acting against the Taliban and helping the US in its actions against Al Qaeda.

Thus, India finds itself in an unenviable position. It is not in a position to make the US and the rest of the Western world act against Pakistan for its inaction against the LeT. At the same time, it is not in a position to act by itself because it has denied to itself a deniable retaliatory capability ever since the fatal decision taken by Inder Gujral, the then Prime Minister, in 1997 to wind up any retaliatory capability as a mark of unilateral gesture to Pakistan — despite remonstrations by senior officers of our security bureaucracy that Pakistan has never been known to appreciate and reciprocate such unilateral gestures. The Pakistani leaders — political or military — know the constraints on India and are taking full advantage of them to persist with their present policy of seeming to act against the LeT without actually acting against it.

The original mistake was committed by Gujral, AB Vajpayee and Manmohan Singh, who followed him, could have reversed it, but they chose not to lest they have problems in our relationship with the US.

One of the major problems faced by us in dealing with the LeT's acts of terrorism in different parts of the country has been due to the failure of our political leadership and the Ministry of External Affairs to make it clear to the world through facts and figures — and not through rhetoric — that the LeT's acts have a much larger agenda and have no longer much to do with the Kashmir issue. Unfortunately, Pakistan has once again almost succeeded in making the US and the UK look at the LeT activities and at 26/11 through the Kashmir prism.

The Mumbai terrorist strike — the attacks on Israelis and other Jewish people, the targeted killings of nationals of countries having troops in Afghanistan, attacks on Western businessmen, etc — clearly illustrated the global agenda of the LeT, but our political leadership and diplomacy failed to clearly draw attention to its much larger agenda. As a result, we are once again seeing references to the so-called linkages between the Kashmir issue and the LeT's acts of terrorism. Pakistan has profited from our inaction or inept action.

We still do not have a coherent policy to deal with Pakistan, which has been a State-sponsor of terrorism in Indian territory and with Bangladesh which acts as a facilitator. Our approach to Pakistan's sponsorship continues to be marked by the "kabhi garam, kabhi naram" (sometimes hard, sometimes soft) syndrome. One of the reasons why Indira Gandhi decided to support the independence movement in the then East Pakistan was because the ISI was giving sanctuaries to the terrorists and insurgents in the Chittagong Hill

Tracts (CHT). The creation of Bangladesh ended this sponsorship in 1971, but it was revived by the intelligence agencies of Pakistan and Bangladesh after the assassination of Sheikh Mujibur Rehman in 1975. We are still struggling to cope with it.

One of the lessons of the post-World War history of State-Sponsored terrorism is that it never ends unless the guilty state is made to pay a prohibitive price. STASI, the East German intelligence service, was behind much of the ideological terrorism in West Europe. The collapse of communism in East Germany and the end of STASI brought an end to this terrorism. The intelligence services of Libya and Syria were behind much of the West Asian terrorism and the Carlos group, then living in Damascus, played a role in helping ideological groups in West Europe. The US bombing of Libya in 1986, the strong US action against Syria, which was declared a State-sponsor of terrorism and against Sudan, where Carlos shifted from Damascus, and the prosecution and jailing, under US pressure, of two Libyan intelligence officers for their complicity in the bombing of a Pan Am plane off Lockerbie on the Irish coast in 1988 brought an end to state-sponsorship of terrorism by Libya and Sudan. Syria has stopped sponsoring terrorism against the US, but continues to do so against Israel.

There are any number of UN resolutions and international declarations declaring state-sponsored terrorism as amounting to indirect aggression against the victim state. Unfortunately, there has been no political will in India to make Pakistan and Bangladesh pay a heavy price for their sponsorship of terrorism against India. Once a firm decision based on a national consensus is taken that the time has come to make Pakistan and Bangladesh pay a price, the question as to which organization should do it and how will be sorted out. The problem is not that we don't have an appropriate organization, but we don't have the will to act against Pakistan and Bangladesh.

We must take action instead of depending on the US or other members of the international community to do so. Every country is interested in protecting the lives and property of only its own citizens. This is natural. It is the responsibility of the Government of India and the States to protect the lives and property of our nationals.

THE ATTITUDE OF THE OBAMA
ADMINISTRATION

Despite differences over strategies and tactics in the fight against global jihadi terrorism, there has been a convergence of views between the previous administration of George Bush and the present administration of President Barack Obama as to what should be the ultimate objective of the US' war against global terrorism. They are both agreed that the ultimate objective should be to prevent another 9/11 in the US homeland by Al Qaeda and an act of catastrophic terrorism involving either the use of weapons of mass destruction (WMD) material or devastating attacks on the critical infrastructure.

In their view, of all the terrorist organizations operating from Pakistani territory, only Al Qaeda has the capability for launching another 9/11 in the US homeland and for organizing an act of catastrophic terrorism. Hence, the first priority of the Bush administration was to the war against Al Qaeda and the Taliban, its ideological ally. This priority continues under Obama too. During the election campaign, Obama's criticism of the policies of Bush was not because of the focus on the war against Al Qaeda and the Taliban, but because of what he looked upon as the inadequacy of that focus as illustrated by the perceived failure of the Bush administration to have Osama bin Laden and his No.2 Ayman Al-Zawahiri killed or captured and the sanctuaries of Al Qaeda in the Pakistani tribal belt destroyed.

He attributed the inadequacy of that focus and the failure of the Bush Administration to destroy or even seriously weaken Al Qaeda to what he looked upon as the unnecessary US involvement in Iraq, which took resources and attention away from the war against Al Qaeda in the Pakistan–Afghanistan region. According to him, the real threat to the US homeland came from the Pakistan–Afghanistan region and not from Iraq and hence there should have been no diversion of the attention and resources from there. He said during the election campaign: "We are fighting on the wrong battlefield. The terrorists who attacked us and who continue to plot against us are resurgent in the hills between Afghanistan and Pakistan. They should have been our focus then. They must be our focus now." In a speech at the Wilson Centre in Washington DC on August 1, 2007, he said: "When I am President, we will wage the war that has to be won…The first step must be getting off the wrong battlefield in Iraq, and taking the fight to the terrorists in Afghanistan and Pakistan."

Another point on which there has been a convergence between the views of the two is over the importance of Pakistan in the war against global terrorism. Both feel that the war against Al Qaeda and the Taliban cannot be won without the co-operation of Pakistan, which essentially means the Pakistani Army. Obama said during the campaign: "Success in Afghanistan requires action in Pakistan. While Pakistan has made some contributions by bringing some Al Qaeda operatives to justice, the Pakistani Government has not done nearly enough to limit extremist activity in the country and to help stabilize Afghanistan. I have supported aid to Pakistan in the Senate and… I would continue substantial military aid if Pakistan takes action to root out the terrorists." He also said when Pervez Musharraf was still the President: "If we have actionable intelligence about high-value terrorist targets and President Musharraf won't act, we will. I firmly believe that if we know the whereabouts of bin Laden and his deputies and we have exhausted all other options, we must take them out."

His proclaimed determination to act unilaterally against high-value targets of Al Qaeda in Pakistani territory is no different from the policy pursued by the Bush Administration in the last year of his presidency. Unmanned Predator aircraft of the Central Intelligence Agency (CIA) carried out over 30 strikes on suspected hide-outs of Al Qaeda and the Taliban in Pakistani territory during 2008 as against 10 in 2006 and 2007. These strikes were carried out despite protests by the Pakistan Government and Army and resulted in the deaths of eight middle-level Arab operatives of Al Qaeda. Since assuming office, Obama has stepped up the Predator attacks on suspected Al Qaeda and Taliban hide-outs in Pakistani territory.

However, Obama has avoided specific pronouncements on his willingness to order land-based strikes on the sanctuaries of Al Qaeda and the Taliban in Pakistani territory. Under the Bush administration, the US special forces did try a land-based strike in South Waziristan in September, 2008, which was not successful. It did not launch any more land-based strikes following a furor in Pakistan. While the Asif Ali Zardari Government is avoiding any action to resist the Predator strikes despite its open condemnation of them, there seems to be a fear in Washington that if the US continues to undertake land-based strikes, public pressure could force the Pakistan Government and the Army to resist them resulting in an undesirable confrontation between the armies of the two countries.

Obama faces the same dilemma as Bush faced. The sporadic successes of the Predator strikes alone will not be able to effectively destroy the terrorist infrastructure of Al Qaeda and the Taliban in Pakistani territory. To be effective, land-based strikes would also be necessary. However, the political consequences of repeated land-based strikes would be unpredictable. There is already considerable anger in the tribal belt against the Pakistan army for co-operating — even half-heartedly — with the US in its war against Al Qaeda and the Taliban. How to make up for this unsatisfactory co-operation by the Pakistan Army by stepping up unilateral US covert actions in the Pakistani territory without adding to the public anger against the Zardari Government is the main question. That was the question to which the advisers of George Bush were not able to come up with a satisfactory answer. Even the advisers of Barack Obama do not seem to have an answer to it so far.

No terrorist organization in Pakistan can exist without State complicity if not sponsorship, sanctuaries and funds. Not only Al Qaeda and the Taliban, but also the largely Punjabi terrorist organizations of Pakistan operating against India in Indian territory enjoy these three essential elements of survival in Pakistan. A ground reality not realized in Washington DC is that all the jihadi terrorist organizations based in Pakistan make available to each other the use of their hide-outs, sanctuaries and training centres. One recently saw the instance of Rashid Rauf of the JeM being killed in a Predator strike on an Al Qaeda hide-out. There have been reports in the Pakistan media of two Punjabi terrorists belonging to what they have described as the Punjabi Taliban being killed in a Predator attack on an Al Qaeda vehicle in South Waziristan on January 1, 2009. The Predator strike targeted and killed Osama al-Kini alias Fahid Mohammad Ally Masalam, described as responsible for Al Qaeda operations in Pakistan, including the bombing of the Marriott Hotel in Islamabad on September 21, 2008, and his No. 2 Sheik Ahmed Salim Swedan. Both were Kenyan nationals. In addition to the two of them, the Predator strike also reportedly killed two members of the JeM, who were also in the same vehicle. One would recall that in March, 2002, Abu Zubaidah, the Palestinian member of Al Qaeda, was caught in a hide-out of the Lashkar-e-Toiba (LeT) in Faislabad in Pakistani Punjab.

From such instances, it should be clear that one cannot make a distinction between sanctuaries of Al Qaeda, those of the Taliban and those of the anti-India organizations. All sanctuaries have to be attacked and destroyed irrespective of to which organization they belonged. The Bush Administration was not prepared to follow such a clear-cut policy and tried to make an operational distinction between anti-US terrorism and anti-Indian terrorism. Pakistan fully exploited this ambivalence.

From the various statements of Obama and his advisers, there is not much reason for India to hope that this ambivalence would disappear under him. The double standards vis-a-vis anti-US and anti-India terrorism, which have been the defining characteristics of US counter-terrorism policies since 1981, will continue to come to the rescue of Pakistan. It would be futile for India to expect any major change under Obama.

President Barack Obama's new comprehensive Af–Pak strategy unveiled on March 27, 2009, to deal with a mix of cancerous problems might impress and enthuse the new Internet generation with which Obama feels comfortable, but not Indian professionals in terrorism with their feet firmly on the ground in this region. These problems arise from the continuing old Islamic insurgency of the 1980s vintage in Afghanistan, the new post-Lal Masjid raid Islamic insurgency in Pakistan, the continuing jihadi terrorism with many faces — anti-West, anti-Indian, anti-Afghan, anti-Israeli, anti-Russian, anti-Chinese, anti-infidels and anti-apostates — from sanctuaries and breeding grounds in Pakistan and the continuing spread of radical ideas justifying the use of terrorism from the madrasas of Pakistan.

Obama and his advisers suffer from the same prescriptive deficiency as their predecessors. This deficiency arises from their tendency to mix facts with illusions. The facts were as clear to Bush and his advisers as they are now to Obama and his advisers. These are the existence in the Pakistani territory of the sanctuaries of Al Qaeda, the Pashtun Taliban and the Punjabi Taliban organizations with the Lashkar-e-Toiba (LeT) and the Jaish-e-Mohammad (JeM) in the forefront and the role of the Pakistan Army and its ISI in nursing them to serve what they perceive as Pakistan's strategic interests.

The prescriptive part of Obama's strategy is as full of illusions as the strategy of Bush was. There is a common root cause for the illusions of the two Administrations. The root cause is their inability to understand that the Pakistani military-intelligence establishment has convinced itself that Pakistan, which had lost its strategic relevance in the immediate aftermath of the end of the cold war, has acquired a new strategic importance. This is thanks to the terrorists of various hues operating from its territory and its nuclear arsenal. The continued existence of these terrorists is in its interest. Action against terrorism when unavoidable, support for terrorism when possible. That is its policy. It has been using its nuclear arsenal not only in an attempt to intimidate India and deter it from retaliating for terrorist strikes in Indian territory, but also to deter the US and the rest of the West from exercising too much pressure on it to deal with the terrorist sanctuaries in its territory.

Unless the mind of the Pakistani military and intelligence officers is disabused of this belief and they are made to co-operate with the international community in destroying the terrorist infrastructure in its territory, no strategy is going to work in ending jihadi terrorism bred in Pakistan. The major deficiency in the prescriptive analysis of Obama arises from his naive assumption that Pakistan can be made to co-operate more effectively against terrorism through a basket of incentives — more military and economic assistance, more training, an emphasis on the continuing importance of Pakistan even after the war on terrorism is over, etc.

Bush too hailed Pakistan as a frontline ally in the war against terrorism and provided it with various lollipops — over US$ 10 billion in military and economic aid since 9/11, dual-use weapons and equipment which could be used against the terrorists as well as against India and a willingness to close the eyes to Pakistan's sins of commission and omission against India so long as it acted against terrorism directed at the US. These lollipops failed to make the regime of Pervez Musharraf co-operate sincerely against Al Qaeda and the Taliban. These incentives could not prevent the Neo Taliban of Afghanistan from staging a spectacular come-back from sanctuaries in Pakistan and Al Qaeda and its associates from organizing acts of terrorism in different parts of the world.

The lessons from the failure of Bush's strategy were: Firstly, a policy based only on incentives will not work in the case of an insincere state such as Pakistan. Secondly, a policy which makes a distinction between terrorism directed against the US and terrorism directed against India and the rest of the world will be ineffective. Thirdly, the fear of exercising too much pressure on Pakistan lest the State collapse and its nuclear arsenal fall into jihadi hands is exploited by Pakistan to prevent the ultimate success of the war against terrorism.

One was hoping — on the basis of the statements by him during his election campaign — that Obama would have factored these lessons into the formulation of his new strategy. Surprisingly, he has not. The same old policy of incentives and nothing but incentives is sought to be pursued under the garb of a so-called new strategy. The only new feature is the emphasis on the benchmarks of implementation which will determine the continued availability of the incentives to Pakistan at every stage. The only disincentive with which Pakistan has been confronted is the risk of the incentives drying up if it is seen as dragging its feet in its co-operation in the fight against terrorism.

Obama's strategy — like the one of his predecessor — is marked by a fear of punishing Pakistan if it does not change its policy of using terrorists to advance its own strategic agenda. The reluctance to punish Pakistan if it continues to be insincere in dealing with terrorism originating from its territory arises from the fear that too much pressure on Pakistan and a policy of punitive measures might push Pakistan into the arms of the jihadis or might result in a collapse of the Pakistani State with unpredictable consequences. The US must rid itself of this fear and make it clear to Pakistan that, if the worst comes to the worst, the world is prepared to face the eventuality of a failed Pakistan. A failed Pakistan may be a disaster for the people of Pakistan, but not necessarily for the rest of the world.

It is important to constitute a contact group to work out alternative strategies with incentives as well as disincentives, with rewards as well as punishments. Such a contact group must be only of the victims of terrorism. A contact group, which seeks to bring together the victims of terrorism as well as the perpetrator, will be a non-starter.

Obama's strategy has three components — a counter-insurgency component for Afghanistan, a counter-terrorism component for use in Pakistan and a counter-radicalization component for use in the entire Af–Pak region. It is a mix of military and political measures. While the military measures will be largely implemented by the US and other NATO powers plus Australia, the regional role of countries such as India, China and Iran is sought to be restricted to the political component. They will have no say in the way the military measures are implemented.

The US expectations that the international community will co-operate in implementing the unilaterally worked out US strategy can be belied because the strategy offers no end in sight to the wave of terrorism of Pakistani origin faced by them. This is particularly true of India. Even though the strategy projects Al Qaeda and its associates operating from sanctuaries in Pakistan as posing a threat to the world as a whole, its objective is limited to preventing another 9/11 in US territory mounted from this region. It does not pay equal attention to the concerns of India and other countries. The strategy is, therefore, unlikely to excite professionals in India.

NEED FOR A COMPREHENSIVE ENQUIRY

We have had enquiries in the past into national security lapses and disasters such as our humiliation at the hands of China in 1962, intelligence failures during the Indo–Pak war of 1965 and the revolt in Mizoram in 1966, the security failures resulting in the assassinations of Indira Gandhi in October, 1984 and Rajiv Gandhi in May, 1991, and our being taken by surprise by the Pakistan Army in the Kargil heights in 1999.

The report of the enquiry into the Chinese occupation of our territory was never released to the public, but we do know that many of the actions taken by the Government of India post-1962 for revamping our national security management were the result of the deficiencies identified during the enquiry. Similarly, the reports of the enquiries into the lapses during the 1965 war and the Mizo uprising were not released to the public, but we do know that the creation of the Research & Analysis Wing (R&AW) was a result of these enquiries. The reports of the other enquiries were released to the public by the Governments of Rajiv Gandhi, Narasimha Rao and Atal Behari Vajpayee.

Since 2000 the world has seen a series of major terrorist strikes — the attack on the US naval ship USS Cole off Aden in October, 2000, 9/11 in the US, the explosion in Bali in October 2002, the Madrid explosions in March 2004 and the London explosions in

July, 2005. Those terrorist strikes were followed by detailed enquiries ordered by the Government in power in order to identify deficiencies and faults, which enabled the terrorists to succeed. Follow-up action was taken to see that similar acts of negligence were not repeated in future and that identified deficiencies were rectified. The conclusions of the enquiries were discussed by their respective legislatures.

On February 27, 2008, Mas Selamat Kastari, said to be a leader of the Singapore branch of Jemaah Islamiyah (JI), escaped from a high security detention centre of Singapore. The escape of this dreaded terrorist created alarm and concern in Singapore about the state of their security agencies. Prime Minister Lee Hsien Loong assured the Parliament and the public that he would see that a thorough enquiry was held to find out how he escaped, to identify the acts of negligence and take necessary follow-up action. He promised that there would be no cover-up and that the enquiry report would be released to the public and discussed in Parliament. He kept his assurance.

The 26/11 terrorist strike caused such an alarm that some leading think-tanks of the world such as the Rand Corporation of the US brought out detailed studies on the incident. The Homeland Security Committees of the US Congress held detailed sessions on the incident for which they invited leading experts to give their assessment of the incident. The conclusion of some of these studies was that India neither had the required preventive capability nor the retaliatory capability to deal satisfactorily with incidents of this nature and hence, one cannot rule out repeats of Mumbai style attacks.

One would have expected the Governments of India and

Maharashtra to order a joint comprehensive and independent enquiry similar to the enquiries held in our own country in the past and similar to those held in other countries since 2000 to identify the sins of commission and omission and the weak points in our counter-terrorism management and to take follow-up action. Unfortunately, the Government of India focused largely on Pakistan's involvement in the strike and avoided any independent enquiry into its own responsibility and that of the Government of Maharashtra, which enabled the ISI and the LeT to succeed in such a spectacular manner.

The Government of India was successful in avoiding a comprehensive enquiry because the Bharatiya Janata Party (BJP) leadership and the other opposition parties, whose responsibility it was to see that there was no cover-up, failed to exercise this responsibility. By their confused inaction, the BJP and other opposition parties played into the hands of the Government and unwittingly facilitated its cover-up exercise. Nobody asked searching questions about our own failures at New Delhi as well as in Mumbai.

While the Government of India successfully avoided any enquiry, the Government of Maharashtra did order an enquiry into the role of the Mumbai police. It set up a two-member enquiry committee consisting of RD Pradhan, an officer of the IAS cadre of Maharashtra, who had served as the Union Home Secretary, and V Balachandran, an officer of the IPS cadre of Maharashtra, who had served for two decades in the R&AW and retired in June, 1995, as a Special Secretary. The enquiry committee completed its work within about four months and submitted its report to the State Government. Unfortunately, public expectations that at least a suitably edited version of the report would be released to the public and discussed in the State Assembly have been belied. The Government of Maharashtra has classified the report and declined to release it to the public. One of the grounds cited for its decision was that the criminal case relating to the attack is subjudice. This was an untenable argument. The reports of the enquiries into the assassinations of Indira Gandhi and Rajiv Gandhi were released despite the two cases being subjudice. Their release did not affect the successful prosecution of the accused.

This was what the Vajpayee Government did in respect of the enquiry report by the Kargil Review Committee, headed by K Subramanyam, the strategic analyst, who was at that time the Convenor of the National Security Advisory Board. There was a wide dissemination of the report and its critical findings. The report was even handed over to a publishing house by the National Security Council Secretariat for publishing it as a book. As a follow-up, the Government also set up a number of Special Task Forces to look into various aspects of national security management such as internal security, border security management, higher defence management and the revamping of the intelligence set-up. An exercise for strengthening national security management on the basis of the recommendations of these task forces was undertaken. Details of the recommendations of all the task forces except the one on the intelligence set-up were released to the public.

Anybody who had watched TV during those three horrible days and read everything that was available to read about the terrorist strike would have noticed that there were apparent lapses which made the strike possible. According to sections of the New Delhi-based national newspapers, intelligence was available, but not complete and continuous. Two reports in September, none in October and one just before the strike. The follow-up action even on the available intelligence was ill-co-ordinated. Emergency response after the strike left much to be desired. There were complaints about inadequate and unsatisfactory protective equipment. The quality of the operational leadership at the counter-terrorism nodal points was criticized. There was an inadequate culture of joint action by various agencies responsible for counter-terrorism.

In his statement to the Lok Sabha after taking over as the Home Minister after the Mumbai attack, P Chidambaram admitted that the responsibility for follow-up action on even the available intelligence was diffused. It must be said to his credit that even though a formal enquiry of an independent nature was not held, he apparently made his own in-house enquiry to determine the deficiencies and correct them. He has tightened up our internal security management system and has been taking active interest in ensuring that the system would function as it should. The fact that an independent enquiry was not held does not mean that a comprehensive in-house exercise was not undertaken to identify and correct deficiencies.

But the public of this country and its legislators have a right to know what went wrong and why. The national security management system is funded by the tax-payers' money. When a terrorist strike takes place, it is their lives and those of their relatives that are affected. By denying the public knowledge of the acts of commission and omission, the political leadership is denying the public and the opposition an opportunity to judge whether the tax-payers' money allocated for counter-terrorism is being spent efficiently. The successful functioning of the national security management system depends not only on the quality of the various components of the system, but also on the co-operation which it is able to get from the public. The readiness of the public to co-operate will depend on the system's credibility in the eyes of the public. If the public is kept in the dark, how can it have the required confidence in the system? Today's terrorism is trans-national. Our ability to deal with it depends not only on our capabilities, but also on the co-operation received from other countries. If the others find that we do not have the moral courage to look into our deficiencies and admit them, what incentive will they have to improve their co-operation with us?

In the light of this, we should have followed the example of other countries and held a comprehensive and independent enquiry, different from an in-house enquiry. One was surprised to note that Chidambaram firmly rejected on June 5, 2009, the demand of LK Advani, the leader of the opposition, for such an enquiry. In an interview to some journalists, he gave the following reasons for his rejecting the demand: Firstly, the demand was belated as it came six months after the terrorist attack. Secondly, the Vajpayee Government did not hold an enquiry into the hijacking of an aircraft of the Indian Airlines by some terrorists to Kandahar in December 1999 and into the attempted attack on the Indian Parliament in December, 2001.

The attack on the Parliament was not an instance of security failure. It was an instance of security success. That was why the terrorists did not succeed. Kandahar was an instance of failure by the then Government. An enquiry should have been held, but the fact that no enquiry was held by the BJP-led Government should not be cited as a ground for not holding an independent enquiry into the Mumbai attack.

Chidambaram was right in pointing out the belated nature of the BJP demand, but this should not have been allowed to stand in the way of a comprehensive and independent enquiry, which would have been in the national interest. I have been pointing out since 2004 that one of the reasons for things going wrong in counter-terrorism management in our country is the lack of activism by the relatives of the victims of terrorist strikes. It was the activism of the relatives of the victims which ensured a thorough enquiry in the US, the UK and other countries. One saw on TV the way the relatives of the victims by rotation attended the hearings of the Congressional committees on the 9/11 strikes and the interest which they took in ensuring that the recommendations of the National Commission were implemented. Unfortunately, in our country, that kind of activism is not there. The Governments are consequently able to get away with their stonewalling.

While the Governments of India and Maharashtra have avoided sharing with the Indian public and legislators the lessons drawn from the 26/11 Mumbai attack, the Department of Homeland Security of the US had prepared a detailed list of the lessons drawn and widely shared it with the public and important private sector companies.

A detailed statement on the subject was made by Under Secretary Charles Allen before the Senate Committee on Homeland Security and Governmental Affairs on January 8, 2009. The text of his testimony is given in Annexure I.

NEED FOR SMART COUNTER-TERRORISM

The 26/11 attack has been the subject of study by the intelligence and security agencies of many countries in order to examine whether the modus operandi (MO) used by the terrorists in Mumbai called for any changes in the counter-terrorism strategies adopted by them. The US Senate Committee on Homeland Security held a detailed hearing in order to understand how and why the terrorists succeeded in Mumbai and how to prevent such incidents in the US. It was terrorism of a conventional nature rendered smarter by modern communications equipment and a good understanding of the way modern media operates. Counter-terrorism failed in Mumbai because it was not as smart as the terrorists were. Smart counter-terrorism is the need of the hour. That is the primal lesson from Mumbai.

The Mumbai attack caused concern right across the international counter-terrorism community not because the terrorists used a new MO, which they had not used in the past, but because they used an old MO with destruction multiplier effect provided by modern communications equipment and lessons drawn from the commando courses of regular armed forces.

There were 166 fatalities in the sea-borne commando-style attack in Mumbai. Only five of them were caused by explosives. The remaining were caused by hand-held weapons (assault rifles and hand-grenades). There had been commando-style attacks with hand-held weapons by terrorists in the Indian territory even in the past, but most of those attacks were against static security guards outside important buildings such as the Parliament House in New Delhi, the US Consulate in Kolkata, a temple in Ahmedabad, etc.

The 26/11 attack was the first act of mass casual terrorism by the jihadi terrorists against innocent civilians using hand-held weapons. The previous two acts of mass casualty terrorism with fatalities of more than 150 were carried out with timed improvised explosive devices (IEDs) — in March 1993 and in July 2006, both in Mumbai.

The increasing use of IEDs by the terrorists since 9/11 had led to strict anti-explosive checks even by private establishments. The killing with IEDs tends to be indiscriminate with no way of pre-determining who should be killed. Moreover, the publicity earned from IED attacks tends to be of short duration. As was seen during the attack on the Parliament House in December, 2001, the visual impact of TV-transmitted images of attacks with hand-held weapons as they were taking place tended to be more dramatic. In an attack with hand-held weapons, the terrorists can pre-determine whom they want to kill.

In Mumbai, 80 people were killed in the terrorist attacks in two hotels and at Narriman House and 86 persons in public places such as the main railway terminus, a hospital, a cafe, etc. Fifteen members of the security forces were killed by the two terrorists moving around with hand-held weapons in public places, but only three members of the security forces were killed during the intervention in the two hotels and the Narriman House. The attacks in some of the public places by the two terrorists on the move lasted about an hour, but caused more fatalities. The static armed confrontations in the hotels and the Narriman House lasted about 60 hours, but caused less fatalities. The static armed confrontations got the terrorists more publicity than the attacks by the two terrorists on the move in public places. By the time TV, radio and other media crew came to know about what was happening in public places and rushed there, the attacks were already over. In the hotels and the Narriman House, the media crew were able to provide a live coverage of almost the entire confrontation. Mrs Margaret Thatcher, the former British Prime Minister, had once described undue publicity as the oxygen of terrorists. The terrorists in Mumbai had 60 hours of uninterrupted oxygen supply.

Within a few hours of the start of the confrontation, the security staff of the hotels reportedly switched off the cable transmissions to the rooms. The terrorists were, therefore, not in a position to watch on TV what was happening outside, but their mobile communications enabled them to get updates on the deployments of the security forces outside from their controllers in Pakistan who, like the rest of the world, were able to watch on their TVs what was happening outside. This could have been prevented only by jamming all mobile telephones. Such jamming could have proved to be counter-productive. Of course, it would have prevented the terrorists from getting guidance and updates from their controllers in Pakistan. At the same time, it might have prevented the security agencies from assessing the mood and intentions of the terrorists and could have come in the way of any communications with the terrorists if the security agencies wanted to keep them engaged in a conversation till they were ready to raid.

The Mumbai attack poses the following questions for examination by all the security agencies of the world:

- Presently, the security set-ups of private establishments have security gadgets such as door-frame metal detectors, anti-explosive devices, closed-circuit TV, etc, but they do not have armed guards. It would not be possible for the police to provide armed guards to all private establishments. How can one strengthen the physical security of vulnerable private establishments and protect them from forced intrusions by terrorists wielding hand-held weapons?

- What kind of media control will be necessary and feasible in situations of the type witnessed in Mumbai? This question had also figured after the Black September terrorist attack on Israeli athletes during the Munich Olympics of 1972. Since then, the position has become more difficult due to the mushrooming of private TV channels and private FM radio stations.

- How can one ensure that mobile telephones do not unwittingly become a facilitator of on-going terrorist strikes without creating operational handicaps for the security agencies? The Israelis, who had taken military action against the Hamas in Gaza, had severely curtailed media access to Gaza. The Hamas sought to overcome this by having visuals of the fighting transmitted to foreign TV channels through mobiles. Copy-cats of this are likely in future.

Smart counter-terrorism has four components — prevention through timely and precise intelligence, prevention through effective physical security, crisis or consequence management to limit the damage if prevention fails and a capability for deniable retaliation if the terrorists operate from the territory of another State. In Mumbai, intelligence was available, but considered inadequate by the police and the Navy/Coast Guard, physical security by the police and the security establishments of the targeted places was deficient, coastal surveillance by the police and the Coast Guard was weak, the consequence management by the National Security Guards (NSG) and others was criticized as tardy and lacking in co-ordination and deniable retaliatory capability was not available.

P Chidambaram initiated certain measures such as enhancing the powers of the police, setting up a National Investigation Agency (NIA) to investigate certain types of terrorism cases and the creation of regional hubs of the NSG in order to reduce delays in response as had allegedly occurred in Mumbai. These are the starting blocks of a revamped counter-terrorism strategy and apparatus, but much more needs to be done.

Just as terrorists are constantly evolving in their thinking and ideology, in their educational background and skills, and in their modus operandi, so too the counter-terrorism strategy of the State actors has also been evolving to meet the threats posed by them. Before 1967, counter-terrorism was seen largely as the responsibility of the Police and the civilian intelligence agencies. After the terrorist organizations took to aviation terrorism involving aircraft hijackings and blowing up aircraft in mid-air as one of their modus operandi, the need for special intervention forces trained by the army was felt. After a surge in acts of terrorism against Israeli nationals and interests in Israel and outside after the Arab–Israeli war of 1967, counter-terrorism in Israel acquired an increasingly military dimension with the role of the police subordinated to that of the armed forces.

This trend towards the increasing militarization of counter-terrorism acquired a further momentum after vehicle-borne suicide bombers, suspected to be from the Hezbollah, blew themselves up outside the barracks of the US Marines and the French paratroopers then deployed as part of an international peace-keeping force in Beirut killing 241 US servicemen and 58 French Paratroopers on October 23, 1983. It was after this incident that the US started talking of a strategy to combat terrorism instead of a strategy to wage a campaign against terrorism. Al Qaeda's attack against the US naval ship USS Cole in Aden in October, 2000, and the subsequent discovery of the plans of Al Qaeda to indulge in acts of maritime terrorism in ports and in choke points such as the Strait of Gibraltar and the Malacca Strait to disrupt international trade and the flow of energy supplies and to damage the global economy gave a naval dimension to counter-terrorism.

Even long before 9/11, counter-terrorism had acquired a scientific and technological dimension due to the increasing use by terrorists of improvised explosive devices (IEDs), but this dimension was restricted to detecting the presence of IEDs and neutralizing them. This S&T dimension has since grown in importance due to the attempts of Al Qaeda to acquire weapons of mass destruction (WMD) material and its proclaimed readiness to use them, if necessary, to protect Islam. This dimension has further expanded due to apprehended threats to critical information infrastructure that could arise from terrorists or hackers helping terrorists, who are adept in the use of information technology for destructive purposes.

Before 1967, terrorism was largely a uni-dimensional threat to individual lives and property. It has since evolved into a multi-dimensional threat to the lives of large numbers of people, to the economy and to the critical information infrastructure. It is no longer viewed as a purely police responsibility. It is the responsibility of the police, the armed forces, the scientific and technological community and the experts in consequence management such as psychologists, fire brigade and medical personnel and experts in disaster relief and rehabilitation. How to ensure co-ordinated and well-synchronized action by the different elements of the counter-terrorism community and what kind of counter-terrorism architecture is required is the question constantly engaging the attention of national security managers of countries affected by terrorism.

Combating terrorism military-style evolved into a war against terrorism after the 9/11 terrorist strikes in the US Homeland. This had three implications. Firstly, a no-forces barred approach in combating terrorism — whether it be the Army, the Air Force, the Navy, the Police or the Special Forces; secondly, an enhanced leadership role for the armed forces in the war against terrorism; and thirdly, a new criminal justice system to deal with terrorists that not only provided for special laws and special courts, but also enabled the armed forces to deal with foreign terrorists operating against US nationals and interests as war criminals liable to be detained in special military camps such as the one in the Guantanamo Bay and to be tried by military tribunals and not by civil courts. President

Barack Obama has been trying to reverse some of these practices and has initiated action to close the Guantanamo Bay detention centre within a year and to transfer the responsibility for trial to normal courts from military tribunals.

Keeping pace with this evolution of a new strategy to combat terrorism, there has been a simultaneous evolution of the counter-terrorism architecture with the addition of many new elements to this architecture. The two most important elements in the US are the Department of Homeland Security (DHS) and the National Counter-Terrorism Centre. The DHS acts as the nodal point for coordinating all physical security measures against terrorism and all crisis management measures to deal with situations arising from successful acts of terrorism in US territory or on its borders, as well as with natural disasters. While the Department of Defence created in 1947 is responsible for all policy-making and co-ordination relating to US military operations abroad, whether against a State or a non-State adversary, the DHS is responsible for all policy-making and inter-departmental co-ordination relating to internal security and natural disasters. A Homeland Security Council in the White House performs an advisory and policy-making role in respect of internal security and natural disasters.

The Homeland Security Council is structurally similar to the National Security Council, with a Secretariat of its own, which is headed by an official, who is designated as the Adviser to the President for Homeland Security and Counter-Terrorism. Its meetings are chaired by the President and attended by various Cabinet members having responsibilities relating to internal security.

In August 2004, Bush established the National Counter-Terrorism Center (NCTC) to serve as the primary organization for integrating and analyzing all intelligence pertaining to terrorism and counter-terrorism (CT) and to conduct strategic operational planning by integrating all instruments of national power. In December 2004, the Congress incorporated the NCTC in the Intelligence Reform and Terrorism Prevention Act (IRTPA) and placed the NCTC under the supervision of the Director of National Intelligence, a newly-created post to co-ordinate and supervise the functioning of all intelligence agencies of the US.

In the UK, as in the past, the Police and the MI-5, the security service, continue to have a pre-eminent role in counter-terrorism of a classical nature such as acts involving the use of hand-held weapons and IEDs. The Armed forces and the S&T community play an enhanced role only in respect of likely terrorist strikes involving WMD material, aviation and maritime terrorism and terrorism through the Internet.

A long-term Counter-terrorism Strategy in the UK called CONTEST formulated in 2003 has four components — Prevention, Pursuit, Protection and Preparation. Prevention refers to the role of the political leadership in preventing British citizens and residents in the UK from joining terrorist organizations through appropriate measures for redressing grievances and for countering the ideology of the terrorists. Pursuit refers to the responsibility of the intelligence and security services and the police to collect preventive intelligence regarding planned terrorist operations and to disrupt the functioning of terrorist organizations through physical security measures and successful investigation and prosecution of terrorist incidents. Protection refers to the physical security measures required to prevent acts of terrorism based on threat or vulnerability perceptions. Preparation refers to the various agencies being in a state of readiness to meet the consequences of an act of terrorism. This is what we in India call crisis management.

Between 9/11 and July, 2005, in the UK too, as in the US, the military dimension of counter-terrorism tended to acquire a greater importance than before due to the perception that the main threat to the UK would be from foreign-based Al Qaeda elements. This perception changed after the July, 2005, terrorist strikes in London by four suicide bombers, who had grown up in the UK. The Intelligence and Security Committee, a Parliamentary oversight committee that reports to the Prime Minister on the performance of the intelligence agencies, which enquired into the failure to prevent the July, 2005, attacks, concluded that the police and the security agencies had failed to adjust sufficiently quickly to the growth of domestic terrorism. It said: "We remain concerned that across the whole of the counter-terrorism community the development of the home-grown threat and the radicalization of British citizens were not fully understood or applied to strategic thinking."

The counter-terrorism strategy and architecture evolved in the UK emphasize the role of the Police working under the over-all supervision of the Home Secretary. A lesson drawn by the British from the July 2005 terrorist strikes in London is that no counter-terrorism strategy will be effective unless it is supported by the community from which the terrorists have arisen. The importance of police–Muslim community relations for preventing the radicalization of the youth and for de-radicalizing those already radicalized and of police-business community relations in order to motivate and help the business community to protect itself from terrorist strikes on soft targets are now two of the important components of the British counter-terrorism strategy.

Among the new elements in the British counter-terrorism architecture, one could mention the National Counter-Terrorism Security Office (NaCTSO) . The NaCTSO, which is funded and operated by the Association of Chief Police Officers, works on the 'protect and prepare' strand of the government's counter-terrorism strategy. Its aims have been defined as follows:

- raise awareness of the terrorist threat, and spread the word about measures that can be taken to reduce risks and mitigate the effects of an attack;

- co-ordinate security advice through the counter-terrorism security adviser (CTSA) network and monitor its effectiveness;

- build relationships between communities, police and government agencies ; and

- contribute to the national and international counter-terrorism policy

It trains, tasks and coordinates a nationwide network of centrally funded specialist police advisers known as counter-terrorism security advisers (CTSAs). The primary role of these advisers is to provide help, advice and guidance on all aspects of counter-terrorism security to the public. It has developed and published guides on physical security against terrorism in sporting stadia and arenas, shopping centers and bars, pubs and clubs. It has undertaken the preparation of similar guides for other soft targets.

The Israeli Counter-Terrorism Strategy has three components — defensive, operative and punitive. Defensive and operative refer to prevention through timely and precise intelligence and operations to disrupt planned terrorist strikes and punitive refers to retaliation by the State against terrorist organizations and their foreign State or non-State sponsors. No intimidation by terrorists, no succumbing to pressure by terrorists, making the terrorists and their sponsors pay heavily for their acts of terrorism, protection of the lives and property of Israeli citizens at any price and a refusal to be paralyzed into inaction against terrorists due to fears of adverse reactions from the international community are the basic principles underlining the Israeli counter-terrorism strategy.

A Global Counter-Terrorism Strategy adopted by the UN General Assembly on September 8, 2006, laid down that any plan of action against terrorism should have the following four components:

- Measures to address conditions which could be conducive to the spread of terrorism.

- Measures to prevent and combat terrorism.

- Measures to build counter-terrorism capacities and to promote international co-operation.

- Measures to protect human rights and to enforce the rule of law.

Whereas other democracies such as those of the US, the UK and Israel have been facing only terrorism of one or two kinds, India has been facing terrorism of multiple origin with varied objectives and different areas of operation. Our intelligence agencies and security forces have been facing cross-border terrorism and hinterland terrorism; urban jihadi terrorism and rural Maoist terrorism; ideological terrorism, religious terrorism and ethnic or separatist terrorism; indigenous jihadi and pan-Islamic jihadi terrorism; and indigenous and Pakistan and Bangladesh sponsored terrorism. The likelihood of maritime terrorism and WMD threats from Al Qaeda based in Pakistan's tribal belt and cyber terrorism from IT-literate terrorists have added to the complexity of the scenario.

Against this background, India's counter-terrorism strategy has to have a common core with principles applicable to all terrorism and separate modules tailor-made and suited to the different kinds of terrorism that we have been facing. The principles of this common core, some of which are in force even now, are:

- The Police would be the weapon of first resort in dealing with hinterland terrorism of all kinds and the army would be the weapon of only last resort.

- In dealing with cross-border terrorism in J&K and with the ULFA and the tribal insurgents in the North-East, the Army would have the leadership role — with the police operating in the interior areas and the Army operating nearer the borders. The paramilitary forces would be available for assistance to the Police as well as the Army.

- Intelligence collection against hinterland terrorism would be the joint responsibility of the Intelligence Bureau (IB) and the State Police and in the border states of the IB, the Police and the Military intelligence. Intelligence collection regarding the external ramifications of all terrorist organizations would be the responsibility of the R&AW.

- Physical security against hinterland terrorism would be the joint responsibility of the State Police and the central security forces such as the Central Industrial Security Force (CISF). In the border areas, it will be the joint responsibility of the Army, the paramilitary forces and the Police.

- The new mutations of terrorism, which could strike India one day, such as WMD, maritime and cyber terrorism have to be dealt with jointly by the Armed Forces, the scientific community and the police — with the army having the leadership role in respect of WMD terrorism, the Navy/Coast Guard in respect of maritime terrorism and an appropriate S&T organization in respect of cyber terrorism.

- While dealing with jihadi terrorism calls for the strengthening of urban policing, dealing with Maoist terrorism cannot be effective without strengthening the rural policing.

While we should follow a no-holds barred approach to crush terrorists from Pakistan and Bangladesh operating in our territory, our strategy in respect of our own nationals who have taken to terrorism should be nuanced with a mix of the political and security strands.

While we should avoid the pitfalls of over-militarization or Americanization of our counter-terrorism strategy, which would be counter-productive in our country with the second largest Muslim population in the world and with our location in the midst of the Islamic world, we should not hesitate to adopt with suitable modifications the best counter-terrorism practices from the US, the UK and Israel.

Among practices worthy of emulation one could mention empowering the police with special laws, the creation of a central agency for co-ordinated investigation and prosecution of terrorism cases, strict immigration control, strong action to stop illegal immigration and to expel illegal immigrants, action to stop the flow of funds to the terrorists from any sources — internal and external — and the adoption of the concept of an integrated counter-terrorism staff for an integrated analysis of all terrorism-related intelligence and joint action on them. All agencies having counter-terrorism responsibilities should be represented in the staff.

The evolution of our counter-terrorism strategy has been in fits and starts as and when we faced a new kind of terrorism or faced a crisis situation. Similarly, our counter-terrorism community too has grown up in a haphazard manner. Our approach to terrorism has been more tactical than strategic, more influenced by short-term thinking than long-term projections. The time has come to set up a dedicated task force to recommend a comprehensive counter-terrorism strategy. The strategy has to be community-based to draw the support of all communities, political consensus-based to draw the support of all political parties and should provide for a close interaction with the private sector to benefit from its expertise and capabilities and to motivate it to protect itself in soft areas.

In 2004, the Government of Dr Manmohan Singh created two posts of National Security Advisers — one for external security, which was held by the late JN Dixit, and the other for internal security, which was held by MK Narayanan. After the death of Dixit in January 2005, the Government reverted to the previous practice of having a single NSA to deal with internal and external security. This post is now held by Narayanan. A reversion to the 2004 practice of having an NSA exclusively for internal security is necessary for improving our counter-terrorism management.

Another important step should be the reorganization of the Ministry of Home Affairs of the Government of India. Counter-terrorism is one of its many responsibilities. While the trend in other countries has been towards having a single Ministry or Department to deal exclusively with counter-terrorism, our MHA has resisted this trend. In any unified command and control for counter-terrorism, the Ministry responsible for counter-terrorism has to play a pivotal role. The importance of having a single leader for dealing exclusively with internal security, without being burdened with other responsibilities was realized by Rajiv Gandhi and Narasimha Rao. Instead of bifurcating the MHA, Rajiv Gandhi created a post of Minister of State for Internal Security in the MHA to handle all operational matters including waging a joint campaign against terrorism by the Centre and the States. This continued under Narasimha Rao. The time has come to create an independent Ministry of Internal Security.

Inadequacies in our intelligence agencies have remained

unidentified and unaddressed. Every successful terrorist strike speaks of an intelligence failure. There is a lack of co-ordination not only among the agencies at the Centre, but also between the central agencies and those of the state police. How to improve the quantity and the quality of the intelligence flow? How to ensure better co-ordination at the Centre and with the States? Important questions such as these were addressed by the Special Task Force for Revamping the Intelligence Apparatus headed by Shri GC Saxena, former head of the R&AW, appointed by the Atal Behari Vajpayee Government in 2000.

The implementation of its recommendations has not had the desired impact on the ground situation. Why? What further measures are needed? These issues have to be urgently addressed by a dedicated task force on terrorism-related intelligence capabilities.

Preventive physical security is the responsibility of central police forces and the police of different States. While the capability at the centre has improved, it has improved in certain States and declined in certain others. A strong physical security capability can thwart a terrorist strike even in the absence of intelligence. A weak capability may not be able to prevent it even if intelligence is available. Identification of weaknesses in our physical security set-up and action to remove them must receive priority.

Successful investigation and prosecution deter future terrorist strikes. Poor investigation and prosecution encourage terrorism. India has a poor record in successful prosecutions. Effective co-ordination of the police in all the States, the creation of a national data base to which the police of different States can have direct access and the quick sharing of the results of the enquiries and investigations through this data base could improve our record in investigation and prosecution.

How can attacks on soft targets be prevented? This has been a dilemma for all States. Israel, which sees many attacks on soft targets by Palestinian suicide bombers, follows a policy of reprisal attacks by the State on the leaders of the suspected organizations after every attack on a soft target, in order to demonstrate to the terrorists that their attacks on soft targets will not be cost free. It is able to do it because the targets chosen by the State agencies for reprisal attacks are located in the areas under the control of the Palestinian Authority. It does not indulge in reprisal attacks in its own territory. Despite such reprisal attacks by the State agencies, Israel has not been able to stop attacks on soft targets. There is no short-term solution to attacks on soft targets except improvement in the capability of our intelligence agencies to collect timely preventive intelligence. Gradual attrition of organizations indulging in such attacks through arrests and neutralization of their leaders could be a medium and long-term solution. That too would require precise intelligence, which is not always available.

Suicide terrorism is a lethal strategic weapon, to which no State has been able to find an effective response. While suicide terrorism against hard, heavily protected targets can be prevented through strict access control, suicide terrorism against soft targets is difficult to prevent unless the suicide terrorist is accidentally detected or the explosive device fails to function.

About 80 per cent of the acts of suicide terrorism are carried out with explosives. Strict explosives control in order to prevent them from falling into the hands of terrorists can make the problem of suicide terrorism more manageable, but the increasing use of commonly available materials such as nitrogenous fertilizers, cosmetics used by women, etc by the terrorists for fabricating explosives has added to the difficulties of the counter-terrorism agencies in preventing explosive substances from falling into the hands of terrorists. Yet, how to tighten up controls over the purchase, sale and acquisition of explosives and substances capable of being converted into explosives is a question, which needs serious attention. While considerable attention has been paid to devising measures to prevent the proliferation of small arms and ammunition, similar attention has not been paid to explosive substances.

Strategic threat analysis has undergone a significant change since 9/11. Before 9/11, analysis and assessment of threat perceptions were based on actual intelligence or information available with the intelligence and security agencies. 9/11 has brought home to policy-makers the difficulties faced by intelligence agencies, however well-endowed they might be, in penetrating terrorist organizations to find out details of their thinking and planning. This realization has underlined the importance of analysts serving policy-makers constantly identifying national security vulnerabilities, which might attract the attention of terrorists, and suggesting options and actions to deny opportunities for attacks to the terrorists. Vulnerability analysis has become as important as threat analysis.

Strategic analysts can no longer confine themselves to an analysis and assessment of strategic developments of a conventional nature arising from State actors, but should pay equal attention to the strategic impact of non-State actors, such as international or transnational terrorists, crime mafia groups and nuclear proliferators on global security in general and our own national security in particular..

India's record in dealing with terrorism and insurgency is not as negative as it is often projected to be. We have had a successful record in Punjab, Nagaland (partial), Mizoram, Tripura and in Tamil Nadu in dealing with terrorism of Al Umma. Even in Jammu & Kashmir, the ground situation is showing signs of definite improvement.

However, there are two kinds of terrorism/insurgency where our record has been poor till now — the jihadi kind, which is essentially an urban phenomenon outside J&K, and the Maoist (Naxalite) kind, which is essentially a rural phenomenon. We have succeeded where the terrorism or insurgency was a regional phenomenon and was confined to a narrow area. We have not succeeded where the threat was pan-Indian in nature with the network extending its presence to many States in the north and the south.

A pan-Indian threat requires a co-ordinated pan-Indian response at the political and professional levels. Unfortunately, the multiplicity of political parties, the era of coalition and the tendency in our country to over-politicize terrorism come in the way of a pan-Indian political response. The tendency of the intelligence agencies and the police of different States to keep each other in the dark about what they know and not to admit to each other as to what they do not know comes in the way of a pan-Indian professional response. There has been a plethora of reports and recommendations on the need for better sharing and co-ordination, but without any effect on our agencies and the police.

The agencies and the Police are largely responsible for the absence of a co-ordinated professional response, but the political leadership at the Centre and in different States cannot escape their share of responsibility. A determined political leader, who has the national interests in mind, can use a whip and make the agencies and the police co-operate. A political leader whose policies and actions are motivated by partisan and not national interests will come in the way of professional co-operation.

Any cure to the problem of jihadi and Maoist terrorism has to start at the political level. A political leader has to play a dual role. He has to help professionals in taking firm action against the terrorists — whatever be their community and ideology. He has to give them whatever tools they need. At the same time, he has to identify the circumstances and perceptions which drive young Muslims to take to jihadi terrorism and young tribals to take to Maoist terrorism. Anger is one of the common root causes of all terrorism. Unless this anger is addressed, professional handling of the threat alone, however effective, cannot bring about an enduring end to this threat.

An effective political handling has to start with a detailed analysis of the causes of anger and action to deal with them. Our young Muslims, who are taking to jihadi terrorism, are not bothered by issues such as lack of education and unemployment, reservation for Muslims, etc. They are angry at what they consider to be the unfairness to Muslims, which, according to them, is widely prevalent in India. Unsatisfactory political handling of the Muslim youth by all political parties is an aggravating cause of the threat from jihadi terrorism.

Similarly, it is the absence of meaningful land reforms and perceptions of suppression of the tribals by the non-tribals and the administration, which is an important cause of the tribal anger in Central India. It is the responsibility of the political class and the society as a whole to address this. They do not do so and keep nursing an illusion that more and more money, men and equipment for the agencies and the police will end this problem. It won't.

The way we kick around the problem of terrorism like a football blaming everybody else except ourselves can be seen in TV debates and media columns. The same arguments are repeated without worrying over their validity.

Flow of human intelligence about jihadi terrorism is weak because of the post-9/11 phenomenon of global Islamic solidarity and the adversarial relationship between the agencies and the police on the one side and the Muslim community on the other. Feelings of Islamic solidarity prevent even law-abiding Muslims from volunteering to the agencies and the police information about their co-religionists, who have taken to terrorism and from assisting the police in their investigation. The adversarial relationship has resulted in mutual demonization. How to come out of this syndrome is a matter for serious consideration not only by the police and the agencies, but also by the political class and the civil society, including the media.

Once we allow terrorism and insurgencies of different kinds to make their appearance in our society it takes a long time to deal with them. We took 19 years to deal with the Naga insurgency, another 19 years to deal with the Mizo insurgency, 14 years to deal with Khalistani terrorism and about 10 years to deal with Al Umma. The French took 19 years to deal with the terrorism of Carlos and his group. Even after 41 years of vigorous implementation of a no-holds-barred counter-terrorism strategy, Israel is still grappling with the terrorism of the Palestinians and the Hezbollah. The British took over 20 years to bring the Irish Republican Army under control.

The attitude of our political class to terrorism is ambivalent. On the one hand, it is worried — rightly — over this growing threat. On the other, it continues to view this as a vote-catcher. Every political party has been firm in demanding action against terrorism when it is out of power. It becomes soft when it comes to power. That is the bane of our counter-terrorism. Only voter pressure can force the political class to stop exploiting terrorism as an electoral weapon and to start dealing with it as a major threat to national security, which should unite the political class and the civil society.

The jihadi terrorism in our territory has been able to thrive because of the support from the intelligence agencies of Pakistan and Bangladesh. Our anxiety for improved relations with them has been coming in the way of any deterrence to their continued use of terrorism against India. The deterrence has to be in the form of an effective covert action capability, which we should be prepared to use against the terrorist infrastructure in Pakistani and Bangladeshi territory, if left with no other option. The covert action capability, which was reportedly wound up in 1997 out of a misplaced sense of generosity to Pakistan, has to be revived.

In our preoccupation with what is happening and what could happen in Pakistan, we should not overlook the urgent need for having a relook at our physical security architecture in sensitive establishments such as the nuclear establishments, oil refineries, gas production infrastructure, road, rail and air transport, critical information infrastructure, etc. I never tire of repeating that physical security is the most important component of counter-terrorism. In both India and Pakistan, we have a weak culture of physical security. The main reason why the US has been able thus far to prevent a repeat of 9/11 is the strengthening of the physical security apparatus by the newly-created Department of Homeland Security.

What happened at Mumbai — namely, commando-style surprise attacks by small groups of well-trained terrorists wielding lethal hand-held weapons — could happen again in India. There is an urgent need for two actions. Firstly, an audit of the physical security measures at all sensitive establishments — whether run by the Government or the private sector — in order to determine whether any physical security enhancements are called for. There is a need for dividing all sensitive establishments into two categories — those where a single-layer of physical security would be enough and those where a double or multiple-layer of physical security would be necessary. The idea of a double or multiple-layer of physical security is that even if the terrorists manage to beat the outside gate or perimeter security, they will not have a free run of the establishment due to a second or more layers of armed physical security. To counter determined terrorists such as those one saw at Mumbai, a single-layer of physical security may not be sufficient in sensitive establishments.

The second action required is to have a relook at our consequence management capabilities to deal with a situation should, despite revamped physical security, the terrorists manage to have access to sensitive establishments. The consequence management drill should take into account various issues such as control over media coverage, prevention of panic, minimization of damage and lethality, etc. It is important to associate the consequence management set-ups of the States with this exercise because it is ultimately they who would act as the protector of first resort through their consequence management capabilities till there is intervention by the consequence management community of the Government of India.

Situated as we are in the sub-continental region where terrorism will continue to be a fact of life at least for another 10 years or more and keeping in view our ambition of emerging as a major economic power, we just cannot afford to take up the stand that the physical security of the private sector is its responsibility and that the Government's role will be limited to issuing periodic advisories regarding likely threats. The Government has to play a more proactive role in encouraging and helping at least establishments of a strategic nature such as those associated with the tourism industry, the information technology companies, etc in improving their physical security. They already have some capability for checks for explosives, but the methods used by them are primitive and do not take into account dangers from suicide bombers and vehicle-borne suicide terrorists.

Their weakest capability — which is almost non-existent — is in facing a commando-style surprise attack by small groups of terrorists with modern hand-held weapons. The only way of thwarting them is by having well-armed and well-trained guards. Do the present laws allow the employment of such guards? If not, should the laws be modified to permit them to employ such well-armed guards? Who is going to supervise their training and keep them under control to prevent the arms issued to them from finding their way into the hands of terrorists? These are questions, which need urgent attention.

From the point of view of the physical security architecture, the distinction between the public and the private sector is disappearing. Many private companies are already in the fields of oil refining and gas exploration, production and transport. An increasing number of airports are now privately managed. We intend allowing private companies into the field of nuclear power production. The Government cannot evade the responsibility for ensuring that such private establishments have a high level of physical security. There is a need for a joint task force consisting of the representatives of the intelligence and security agencies and professional organizations of private industries such as the FICCI (Federation of Chambers of Commerce and Industries), the CII (the Confederation of Indian Industries), etc as well as representatives of foreign business organizations to go into the question of physical security enhancements for private establishments of strategic significance.

Practically all major private establishments — Indian as well as foreign — have their own physical security set-up. It is important for senior intelligence and security officials at the State and Central levels to regularly interact with them to exchange threat and vulnerability perceptions and ideas as to how to strengthen physical security.

In an important article titled "The Coming Swarm" in the *New York Times* of February 15, 2009, which should be required reading for all our physical security experts, John Acquilla, who teaches in the special operations program at the Naval Postgraduate School at Monterey in California, wrote as follows: "It seems that a new 'Mumbai model' of swarming, smaller-scale terrorist violence is emerging. The basic concept is that hitting several targets at once, even with just a few fighters at each site, can cause fits for elite counter-terrorist forces that are often manpower-heavy, far away and organized to deal with only one crisis at a time. This approach certainly worked in Mumbai. The Indian security forces, many of which had to be flown in from New Delhi, simply had little ability to strike back at more than one site at a time. While it's true that the assaults in Kabul seem to be echoes of Mumbai, the fact is that Al Qaeda and its affiliates have been using these sorts of swarm tactics for several years...How are swarms to be countered? The simplest way is to create many more units able to respond to simultaneous, small-scale attacks and spread them around the country. This means jettisoning the idea of overwhelming force in favor of small units that are not "elite" but rather "good enough" to tangle with terrorist teams. In dealing with swarms, economizing on force is essential. ... For the defense of American cities against terrorist swarms, the key would be to use local police officers as the first line of defense instead of relying on the military. The first step would be to create lots of small counter-terrorism posts throughout urban areas instead of keeping police officers in large, centralized precinct houses. This is consistent with existing notions of community-based policing... At the federal level, we should stop thinking in terms of moving thousands of troops across the country and instead distribute small response units far more widely. Cities, states and Washington should work out clear rules in advance for using military forces in a counter-terrorist role, to avoid any bickering or delay during a crisis. Reserve and National Guard units should train and field many more units able to take on small teams of terrorist gunmen and bombers. Think of them as latter-day Minutemen. Saudi Arabia, Tunisia, Turkey and Yemen all responded to Qaeda attacks with similar "packetizing" initiatives involving the police and armed forces; and while that hasn't eliminated swarm attacks, the terrorists have been far less effective and many lives have been saved."

As already stated, jihadi terrorism in India outside Jammu & Kashmir is essentially an urban phenomenon. We cannot use against it the techniques learnt by us in dealing with the insurgency in the North-East and with Maoist terrorism in Central India. We need a different system of response, which is comprehensive enough to cover all likely targets of strategic significance — whether in the Government or private sector. Even if we do not create an independent Ministry of Internal Security, we should create a separate Department of Physical Security in the Ministry of Home Affairs, which is, inter alia, responsible for counter-terrorism, to act as the nodal agency for all physical security measures on the pattern of the Department of Homeland Security of the US. This newly-created department should interact continuously with its US counterpart to pick its brains and profit from its expertise and experience.

The Government is already reported to have taken some steps for toning up the intelligence collection capability by strengthening the Multi-Agency Centre. Chidambaram, the Home Minister, is reported to have taken action to address the staff and resource constraints faced by the MAC. Even before the Mumbai attack, the National Security Adviser (NSA) had set up a new Task Force headed by Dr SD Pradhan, former Chairman of the Joint Intelligence Committee (JIC), to have a fresh look at measures required for further strengthening intelligence collection and co-ordination in the light of developments since 2000. Inter alia, this Task Force is also expected to address the resource and manpower shortages faced by the intelligence agencies and to remove red tapes in the processing of their proposals in this regard. While these measures would result in short-term improvements in the functioning of the intelligence community, there is a need to think strategically of medium and long-term measures. Such strategic thinking has to be based on the assumption that any significant improvement in our bilateral relations with Pakistan is unlikely in the near future and that Pakistan-sponsored terrorism would continue to be the most serious internal security threat. Such strategic thinking should also take into consideration a scenario where the developing strategic relations between India and the US makes India a target of global terrorist organizations, such as Al Qaeda. To provide a strategic framework for improving our capability for prevention through intelligence, it is necessary to set up a Special Task Force exclusively dedicated to intelligence-driven counter-terrorism to come out with a set of recommendations for this purpose. The piecemeal measures initiated by the Government since the Kargil conflict for improving co-ordination among intelligence agencies have not completely removed all the deficiencies which led to our being taken by surprise by the clandestine occupation of the Kargil heights by the Pakistan Army. Presently, the responsibility for intelligence coordination is with the NSA as recommended by the Saxena Task Force. The time has come to create a post of National Intelligence Coordinator to handle the task of co-ordination on a full-time basis. Like the NSA, he could work under the Prime Minister.

Outside Jammu & Kashmir, the externally-sponsored jihadi terrorists have been focusing mainly on metro cities such as Mumbai (three mass-casualty attacks in March, 1993, July, 2006 and November, 2008), Delhi (two attacks in October, 2005 and September, 2008 plus the unsuccessful attack on the Parliament in December, 2001), Hyderabad (two attacks since 2006) and Jaipur, Ahmedabad and Bangalore (one attack each in 2008). Only Chennai and Kolkata have so far escaped mass casualty attacks. These attacks have, inter alia, the purpose of shaking the confidence of our people as well as foreign investors and businessmen in the capabilities of our counter-terrorism machinery. Future attacks are also likely to be directed at such metro cities, which are the economic nerve-centers. In addition to a national plan for strengthening counter-terrorism, we should have separate tailor-made plans for Delhi, Mumbai, Chennai, Kolkata, Bangalore, Hyderabad, Jaipur and Ahmedabad. These plans should focus on capacity-building through improved manpower and resource availability and better training.

OTHER POINTS FOR ACTION

POINT 1: Set up a National Commission of professionals with no political agenda, in consultation with the Leader of the Opposition, to enquire into all the major terrorist strikes that have taken place Indian territory outside Jammu & Kashmir (J&K) since November, 2007, and task it to submit its report within four months, with no extensions given. Its charter will be not the investigation of the criminal cases arising from these terrorist strikes, but the investigation of the deficiencies and sins of commission and omission in our counter-terrorism agencies at the Centre and in the States, which made these strikes possible.

POINT 2: Make the IB the nodal point for all liaisons with foreign intelligence and security agencies in respect of terrorism, instead of the R&AW. Give the IB direct access to all foreign internal intelligence and security agencies, instead of having to go through the R&AW.

POINT 3: Have a common data base on terrorism shared by the IB and the R&AW directly accessible by authorized officers of the two organizations through a secure password.

POINT 4: Make the Multi-Agency Centre of the IB function as it was meant to function when it was created — as a centre for the continuous identification of gaps and deficiencies in the available intelligence and for removing them and for effective follow-up action.

POINT 5: Revive the covert action capability of the R&AW and strengthen it. Its charter should make it clear that it will operate only on foreign territory and not on Indian territory. Give it specific, time-bound tasks. All covert actions should be cleared and co-ordinated by the R&AW. Other agencies should not be allowed to indulge in covert actions.

POINT 6: The National Security Guards (NSG) was created as a special intervention force to deal with terrorist situations such as hijacking and hostage-taking. Stop using it for VIP security purposes.

POINT 7: Give the police in Delhi, Mumbai, Kolkata, Chennai and Bangalore a special intervention capability to supplement that of the NSG.

POINT 8: After the series of hijackings by the Khalistani terrorists in the early 1980s, Indira Gandhi had approved a proposal for the training of Indian experts in dealing with hostage situations and hostage negotiation techniques by foreign intelligence agencies, which have acknowledged expertise in these fields. The training slots offered by the foreign agencies were largely monopolized by the IB and the R&AW. The utilization of these training slots and the selection of officers for the training should be decided by the NSA — with one-third of the slots going to Central agencies, one-third to the NSG and one-third to the State Police. It is important to build up a core of terrorism and counter-terrorism expertise in all metro towns.

POINT 9: The IB's Multi-Agency Centre should have a constantly updated database of all serving and retired officers at the Centre and in the States, who had undergone overseas training, and also of all serving and retired officers and non-governmental figures who have expertise in terrorism and counter-terrorism so that their expertise could be tapped, when needed.

POINT 10: Strengthen the role of the police stations in counter-terrorism in all major cities. Make it clear to all Station House Officers that their record in preventing acts of terrorism, in contributing to the investigation and prosecution of terrorism-related cases and in consequence management after a terrorist strike will be an important factor in assessing their suitability for further promotion. Revive and strengthen the beat system, revive and intensify the local enquiries for suspicious activities in all railway stations, bus termini, airports, hotels, inns and other places and improve police–community relations.

POINT 11: Adopt the British practice of having counter-terrorism Security Advisers in Police Stations. Post them in all urban police stations. Their job will be to constantly train the PS staff in the performance of their counter-terrorism duties, to improve relations with the communities and to closely interact with owners of public places such as hotels, restaurants, shopping malls, etc and voluntarily advise them on the security precautions to be taken to prevent terrorist strikes on soft targets and to mitigate the consequences if strikes do take place despite the best efforts of the police to prevent them.

POINT 12: Stop using the National Security Council Secretariat (NSCS) as a dumping ground for retired officers, who are favored by the Government. The NSCS cannot be effective in its role of national security management if it is not looked upon with respect by the serving officers. The serving officers look upon the retired officers of the NSCS as living in the past and in a make-believe world of their own, totally cut off from the ground realities of today in national security management. The NSCS should be manned only by serving officers of acknowledged capability for thinking and action.

POINT 13: Strengthen the role of the National Security Advisory Board (NSAB) as a Government-sponsored think tank of non-governmental experts in security matters to assist the NSCS and the NSA. Give it specific terms of reference instead of letting it freelance as it often does. It should be discouraged from undertaking esoteric studies.

POINT 14: Set up a separate Joint Intelligence Committee (JIC) to deal with internal security. Assessment of intelligence having a bearing on internal security requires different expertise and different analytical tools than assessment of intelligence having a bearing on external security. In 1983, Indira Gandhi, then Prime Minister, bifurcated the JIC and created a separate JIC for internal security. Rajiv Gandhi reversed her decision. Her decision was wise and needs to be revived.

POINT 15: Set up a National Counter-Terrorism Centre (NCTC) under the National Security Adviser (NSA) to ensure joint operational action in all terrorism-related matters. It can be patterned after a similar institution set up in the US under Director, National Intelligence after 9/11. The National Commission set up by the US Congress to enquire into the 9/11 terrorist strikes had expressed the view that better co-ordination among the various agencies will not be enough and that what was required was a joint action command similar to the Joint Chiefs of Staff in the Armed Forces. Its tasks should be to monitor intelligence collection by various agencies, avoid duplication of efforts and resources, integrate the intelligence flowing from different agencies and foreign agencies, analyze and assess the integrated intelligence and monitor follow-up action by the Police, the Federal Bureau of Investigation and other concerned agencies. Every agency is equally and jointly involved and responsible for the entire counter-terrorism process starting from collection to action on the intelligence collected. If such a system had existed, post-Mumbai complaints such as those of the Intelligence Bureau (IB) and the Research and Analysis Wing (R&AW) that the advisories issued by them on the possibility of a sea-borne attack by the LeT on Mumbai were not acted upon by the Mumbai Police and the Navy would not have arisen because the IB and the R&AW would have been as responsible for follow-up action as the Mumbai Police and the Navy.

POINT 16: The practice of the privileged direct access to the Prime Minister by the chiefs of the IB and the R&AW, which came into force under Jawaharlal Nehru and Indira Gandhi, should be vigorously enforced. This privileged direct access is utilized by the intelligence chiefs to bring their concerns over national security and over inaction by the agencies responsible for follow-up on their reports to the personal notice of the Prime Minister and seek his intervention.

POINT 17: Set up a task force consisting of three senior and distinguished Directors-General of Police (DGPs) and ask it to come up with a list of recommendations for strengthening the powers of the police in respect of prevention, investigation and prosecution of terrorism-related offences and the capabilities of the Police in counter-terrorism and implement its recommendations. This is the only way of getting round the present political deadlock over the revival of the Prevention of Terrorism ACT (POTA).

POINT 18: Expedite the erection of the border fence on the border with Bangladesh without worrying about opposition from Bangladesh.

POINT 19: Start a crash program for the identification of illegal immigrants from Bangladesh and for deporting them. Ban the employment of immigrants from Bangladesh anywhere in Indian territory.

POINT 20: Strict immigration control is an important part of counter-terrorism. The post–9/11 safety of the US is partly due to the tightening up of immigration procedures and their strict enforcement. Among the best practices adopted by the US and emulated by others are: Photographing and finger-printing of all foreigners on arrival, closer questioning of Pakistanis and persons of Pakistani origin, etc. We have not yet adopted any of these practices. Hotels and other places of residence should be banned from giving rooms to persons without a departure card and without a valid immigration stamp in their passports. They should be required to take photo copies of the first page and the page containing the immigration stamp of the passports of all foreigners and also the departure card stapled to the passport and send them to their local Police Station every morning. All immigration relaxations introduced in the case of Pakistani and Bangladeshi nationals and persons of Pakistani and Bangladeshi origin should be cancelled with immediate effect. The requirement of police reporting by them should be rigorously enforced. It should be made obligatory for all persons hosting Pakistanis and Bangladeshis to report to the local police about their guests. A vigorous drive should be undertaken for tracing all Pakistanis and Bangladeshis overstaying in India after the expiry of their visas and for expelling them.

POINT 21: The MEA's capability for terrorism-related diplomacy should be strengthened by creating a separate Division for this purpose. It should continuously brief all foreign governments about the role of Pakistan and Bangladesh in supporting terrorism in Indian territory and press for action against them.

POINT 22: The Mumbai strikes have revealed serious gaps in our maritime security on our Western coast. This is partly the result of our over-focus on the Look East policy and the neglect of the Look West dimension. This was corrected in the beginning of 2008. Despite this, there are apparently major gaps as seen from an alleged failure by the Naval and Coast Guard authorities to act on the reports of the IB and the R&AW about likely sea-borne threats from the LeT. The identification and removal of the gaps need immediate attention. The Mumbai off-shore oil installations and the nuclear and space establishments on the Western coast are also vulnerable to sea-borne terrorist strikes.

ANNEXURE I

Lessons Drawn by the US from the Mumbai Attacks

"Terrorist Attacks"

Release Date: January 8, 2009

Testimony of Under Secretary Charles Allen before the Senate Committee on Homeland Security and Governmental Affairs, "Lessons from the Mumbai Terrorist Attacks".

Dirksen Senate Office Building

(Remarks as Prepared)

Thank you, Chairman Lieberman, Senator Collins, and Members of the Committee for the invitation to discuss the lessons the Department of Homeland Security (DHS) learned following the recent terrorist attacks in Mumbai, India. I would like to highlight for you our intelligence information sharing efforts regarding these attacks.

The Office of Intelligence and Analysis routinely analyzes and provides information, in conjunction with the Federal Bureau of Investigation (FBI), on overseas terrorist threats and attacks with our state, local, tribal, and private sector partners to assist them in protecting our nation, its vital assets, and citizens. We have analyzed the November 26–30, 2008 Mumbai attacks, where members of a well-armed, and trained terrorist group made a maritime entry into the coastal city and then fanned out to attack multiple locations, including transportation, commercial, and religious facilities. The assailants apparently were familiar with target layouts and security postures, indicating pre-operational planning and surveillance. We continue to analyze the Mumbai attacks as new data become available, and we and the FBI will share this information broadly with our customers to help them protect our nation's citizens and critical infrastructure and to hone our capabilities to respond quickly and decisively to any terrorist attacks on the Homeland. Broadly, the lessons learned thus far can be categorized into prevention and deterrence, and response and recovery.

Prevention and Deterrence

We are reminded that disrupted plots may resurface. Indian authorities apparently arrested a Lashkar-e-Tayyba (LT) operative in February 2008 who carried with him information suggesting Mumbai landmarks, including the Taj Mahal Hotel, had been targeted for surveillance, possibly for a future terrorist operation. Indian authorities shared the information with the hotel owners and the security was bolstered at the Taj Mahal and at several other locations. Some time prior to the attacks, however, security at many of the sites identified in the February 2008 arrests was reduced to more routine levels. It is apparent now that the LT's overall intention to attack Mumbai was not disrupted — LT plotters evidently had delayed their attack plans until a time of their choosing. This is a valuable lesson that we have also learned from the multiple plots planned against New York City, including the World Trade Center Towers, before the September

11 attacks brought the towers down. This lesson appeared to have been repeated in Mumbai. An intelligence informed threat warning and a heightened security posture may have delayed the attack in Mumbai, but LT plotters continued to plan for attacks on Mumbai's financial and entertainment center. DHS and the intelligence and law enforcement communities must remain cognizant that targets identified in previous plots are likely to resurface in the future.

A determined and innovative adversary will make great efforts to find security vulnerabilities and exploit them. The Mumbai attackers entered the city via the sea because they may have believed it was the best route to avoid detection. Sea infiltration permitted the attackers to come ashore with a substantial cache of weapons that might have been detected during a land entry into the city. Terrorists are always seeking to identify weaknesses in our security and exploit them. Vulnerability assessments used to develop security and protective protocols must look closely at our nation's assets from the perspective of the terrorist, vigorously seek the weaknesses that they can exploit, and work tirelessly to minimize if not eliminate those weaknesses.

Security must be unpredictable for the adversary, but predictably responsive to those it is meant to protect. The Mumbai attackers were able to ascertain the routines and vulnerabilities of the security forces at the primary targets during the pre-operational phase. For this reason, it is important to vary security routines and establish capabilities to "surge" security forces, such as we have done in DHS, through the Transportation Security Administration, with our Visual Intermodal Prevention and Response (VIPR) teams. In addition, during the period of heightened security, several of the hotels that were attacked installed security scanning devices. According to open source reporting, some of these devices were not in operation during the attacks, and all security personnel were not properly trained on those devices that did work. Effective training of private sector security personnel and first responders is an essential element of securing our nation's critical infrastructure — 85 percent of which is privately owned. Training of the private sector on detection, deterrence, response and recovery is essential to protecting our homeland. To that aim, my office shares, on a routine basis, intelligence-derived threat information on potential adversaries and their tactics with state and local authorities, and private sector security personnel. This information can be used to develop coordinated public-private response plans and train first responders on how best to respond to various attack methods that may be employed by terrorists so as to better protect personnel and resources.

Target knowledge was paramount to the effectiveness of the attack. The terrorists were able to collect sufficient information on all targets to execute a successful attack. Much of the information they required was accessible through open sources that are readily available in any open society. Hotels, restaurants, and train stations by their nature are susceptible to extensive surveillance activities that might not necessarily draw attention because the public is frequently moving through them. In the Mumbai attacks, during the planning and training stages, the cells reportedly used information from commercial imagery providers as well as pictures and videos from each of the targets acquired by support personnel. Surveillance by terrorist operatives or support personnel represents an opportunity to identify and interdict terrorist operatives. The Department is working, in cooperation with the Office of the Director of National Intelligence (ODNI), the Federal Bureau of Investigation (FBI), and our state, local, tribal, and private sector partners to establish a comprehensive Suspicious Activity Reporting system that is designed to systematically collect and identify possible pre-attack activity.

"Low tech" attacks can achieve terrorist strategic goals — and can be dramatically enhanced by technology enablers. The Mumbai attackers were able to locate precise landing points by using Global Positioning System (GPS) for navigation. The attackers were also able to fend off the Indian response force because they were heavily armed with automatic rifles and grenades — the weapons of a basic infantryman. The group reportedly received extensive training that may have included urban assault operations. In addition, the attackers used wireless communication devices, including satellite and cell phones, to coordinate movement activities, establish defensive positions, repel rescuers, and resist Indian efforts to suppress them. Open source reporting also indicates they monitored press coverage of the attack through wireless communication devices — which may have been taken from hostages — that may have provided some tactical advantages against the Indian rescue forces.

Response and Recovery

Response to a similar terrorist attack in a major US urban city would be complicated and difficult. The chaos the attacks created magnified the difficulty of mounting an appropriate response. First responders, in order to deal with such a crisis, must first and foremost have adequate information on what is occurring, as well as the capability to mount a rapid and effective response that minimizes the impact of the attack. In Mumbai it was not immediately clear to authorities whether there were multiple attack groups or a single group. The attackers were able to exploit the initial confusion because of the indiscriminate firings to move on to new targets. While preparedness training for this type of attack may not have prevented it, the effects likely could have been mitigated and reduced if authorities had been prepared and had exercised responses to terrorist attacks across all levels of government. Within the United States, our national exercises incorporate not only federal interagency participants, but also include regional, state, and local authorities, in order to identify potential gaps in our responses.

A unified command system is of paramount importance if governments are to respond to terrorist attacks quickly and effectively. Within the United States, we have developed the National Response Framework (NRF) and the National Incident Management System (NIMS) that provide us with a unified command system to respond to such attacks as well as natural disasters. This framework, while not a panacea, does provide guidance on organizational roles and responsibilities during response and recovery operations. The NRF and NIMS also provide mechanisms to convey to the public critical information, such as areas to avoid during an incident or the potential for additional attacks in other areas or regions.

Public-private interactions are crucial and must be developed before an incident occurs. Developing these relationships before an incident helps facilitate the flow of information during the crisis and may help ensure the data conveyed to first responders are accurate, such as changes in floor plans or access routes. Within DHS, the

Office of Infrastructure Protection manages many public-private partnerships. Our efforts to build bridges between intelligence analysts and the owners and operators of the private sector that operate most of our critical infrastructures is ongoing and sustained. Furthermore, there are also many programs in operation and under development at the state and local level to expand relationships between owners and operators and first responders.

Threat information must be quickly and accurately conveyed to the public. Accurate information serves to protect the public, reassuring them that the government is responding appropriately to the threat or attack. Information flow must be timely and managed in a manner that prevents the terrorists from potentially benefiting from what the authorities know about the attackers. Within DHS, we have established procedures and protocols to release accurate threat information quickly. These procedures during an incident include a thorough review to ensure protection of sensitive information. We have exercised this process on numerous occasions.

Training exercises that integrate lessons learned are critical. Through various national and state programs, DHS and agencies with homeland security responsibilities have exercised and practiced our coordinated response to terrorist attacks. We have taken the lessons learned in the September 11 attacks and the many attacks that have occurred overseas, and incorporated them into our national planning exercises. We have practiced coordinating responses to multiple attacks across federal, state, local, and tribal authorities. We will incorporate Mumbai-style attacks in future exercises to refine further our response capabilities. We have identified shortfalls and gaps, such as interoperable communications systems and intelligence analytic capabilities at the local level, and are using the DHS grants programs to address those shortfalls.

Lastly, we must protect the attack sites to collect intelligence and evidence to identify the perpetrators. In many instances, it may not be readily apparent which group is responsible. While the preservation of life is paramount, preservation of crime scenes is an important consideration to identify the attackers and hold them accountable. This requires training and experience to execute effectively.

Now, Let me briefly convey the information sharing actions of my Office of Intelligence and Analysis (I&A) — in conjunction with our partners at the FBI — during and after the Mumbai attacks. You also asked that we discuss DHS' information sharing with India following the attack. I respectfully request that we leave discussions of what has specifically been shared for a closed session to protect information the Indian government deems sensitive. I will note, however, that we have been working very closely with the Indian government to provide any information and assistance that we can.

Information sharing with state, local, tribal, and private sector partners is central to the intelligence mission of I&A. As noted earlier, we share this information to better secure our nation's infrastructure and to protect its citizens, by ensuring state, local, and tribal authorities and private sector owners are aware of the threat environment and tactics that may be employed by would-be terrorists. In addition to distribution of unclassified analyses focused on the homeland security implications of the Mumbai attack, I&A

staff also fielded numerous questions from state, local, and tribal authorities and our private sector partners.

Less than 24 hours after the November 26th attacks, I&A, acting jointly with the FBI, released a situational awareness update with the most current, 'For Official Use Only' (FOUO), information. This product, titled Islamic Militant Group Attacks Multiple Locations in Mumbai, India was disseminated broadly to all federal, state, local, tribal, and private sector stakeholders. That same day, November 27, I&A analysts consolidated intelligence regarding the attack tactics and began drafting a report for federal, state, local, tribal, and private sector entities describing the attack and its implications for homeland security. Between November 28 and December 2, I&A analysts provided classified and unclassified briefings on the attacks to private sector organizations, including a teleconference with approximately 250 attendees from the Commercial Facilities Sector Coordinating Council (SCC), the Transportation SCC, the Electric Power SCC, the Partnership for Critical Infrastructure Security, the Federal Senior Leadership Council, the Information Sharing and Analysis Centers Council among others and the Homeland Security State and Local Community of Interest (HS-SLIC) State, Local, and Tribal, and Territorial Government Coordinating Council (SLTTGCC). On December 3, the FBI and I&A published a FOUO Joint Homeland Security Note, Mumbai Attackers Used Commando-Style Assault Tactics, describing our preliminary findings on the terrorist tactics used in Mumbai for federal, state, local, tribal, and private sector partners. I&A also released a FOUO background primer for federal, state, and local officials in early December on the LT terrorist organization. This "Homeland Security Reference Aid" discussed the group's history, leadership, membership, targeting preferences, and homeland nexus. In the weeks following the attacks, I&A has continued to provide classified and unclassified briefings, particularly to the private sector; tailoring presentations for the Nuclear SCC, the Financial Services Sector's SCC and Information Sharing & Analysis Center, and the Financial and Banking Information Infrastructure Committee. Homeland security stakeholders have responded positively to our efforts and, according to I&A intelligence officers in fusion centers nationwide, their state and local counterparts have praised DHS for providing timely, relevant information in the attacks' aftermath. A senior security official at a large private company singled out I&A during a recent address, noting that the timely intelligence information provided by DHS was a "breath of fresh air."

I have touched on a broad range of information on the lessons learned and our information sharing activities in support of state, local, tribal, and private sector partners with information regarding the tragic attacks in Mumbai. DHS is making strong efforts to foster information sharing at all levels of government. We remain committed to implementing the information sharing mandates of the Intelligence Reform and Terrorism Act of 2004, the Homeland Security Act of 2002, and the August 2007 9/11 Commission Act. We do this with full concern for the civil rights, civil liberties, and privacy of all Americans.

Thank you and I look forward to your questions.

ANNEXURE II

Salient Points from the Investigation Report Submitted by the Mumbai Police to the Court before which the Case is being Tried

DURATION OF THE CONSPIRACY

From December 2007 to November 2008. The conspiracy to carry out the terrorist strike was hatched in December 2007 and carried out in November 2008.

Number of Persons in Pakistan Involved in the Conspiracy and their Names

35 names given below.

Prof. Hafeez Mohammad Sayeed

Zaki-ur-Rehman Lakhvi

Abu Hamza

Abu al Kama aka Amjid

Abu Kaahfa

Mujamil alias Yusuf

Zarar Shah

Abu Fahad Ullah

Abu Abdul Rehman

Abu Anas

Abu Bashir

Abu Imran

Abu Mufti Saeed

Hakim Saab

Yusuf

Mursheed

Aakib

Abu Umar Saeed

Usman

Major-General Sahab — Name not known

Kharak Singh

Mohammad Ishfak

Javid Iqbal

Sajid Iftikhar

Col. Saadat Ullah

Khurram Shahdad

Abu Abdurrehman

Abu Mavia

Abu Anis

Abu Bashir

Abu Hanjla Pathan

Abu Saria

Abu Saif-ur-Rehman

Abu Imran

Hakim Sahab.

Number of Pakistani Perpetrators who Sailed to Mumbai and Participated in the Attack

10. Their names are given below.

Group which Moved Round the Area and Kiiled People Indiscriminately in Public Places

(1) Mohammad Ajmal Mohammad Amir Kasab aka Abu Mujahid. Age 21. Resident of village Faridkot in Dipalpur Tehsil, District Okara, Punjab.Pakistan.

(2) Ismail Khan alias Abu Ismail, resident of Dera Ismail Khan, Punjab, Pakistan

Group which Targeted the Taj Mahal Hotel

(1) Hafiz Arshad aka Abdul Rehman Bada aka Hayaji, resident of Multan Road, Punjab, Pakistan.

(2) Javed aka Abu Ali, Resident of district Okara, Punjab, Pakistan.

(3) Shoaib aka Abu Shoheb, resident of Naroval, Shakkar Road, Sialkot, Punjab, Pakistan

(4) Nasir aka Abu Umar, resident of Faislabad, Punjab, Pakistan.

Group which Targeted the Oberoi/Trident Hotel

(1) Abdul Rehman Chhota aka Saakib, resident of Arafwala, Multan Road, Punjab, Pakistan

(2) Fahad Ullah, resident of Ujarashamukam, Dipalpur, Harun Sheikh Kasoor Road, Punjab, Pakistan.

Group which Targeted the Narriman House

(1) Imran Babar aka Abu Aakasha, resident of Multan, Punjab, Pakistan

(2) Nasir aka Abu Umar, resident of Faislabad, Punjab Pakistan

Of the Persons Mentioned Above Amir Kasab Was Captured Alive and is Under Trial. The Other Nine Died During the Operation.

INDIAN MUSLIMS ARRESTED AND PROSECUTED

(1) Fahim Arshad Mohammad Yusuf Ansari aka Abu Jarar aka Sakib aka Sahil Pawaskar aka Sameer Sheikh aka Ahmed Hasan. Age 35. 303 Motilal Nagar, No. 2, M.G.Road, Goregaon, Mumbai.

(2) Sabauddin Ahmed Shabir Ahmed Sheikh aka Saba aka Farhan aka Mubbashir aka Babar aka Sameer Singh aka Sanjiv aka Abu al Kasim aka Iftikhar aka Murshad aka Mohammad Shafik aka Ajmal Ali. Age 24. Address? Post Gandwar, Sakri Police Station via Pandol, District Madhubani, Bihar.

Evidence Against the two Indian Muslims

Ansari collected topographical information relating to the location of the targets, prepared detailed maps and gave them to Sabauddin, who passed them to an LeT operative in Kathmandu, Nepal.

Training in Pakistan of the Pakistani Perpetrators

They were trained in various places in Pakistan and Pakistan-Occupied Kashmir (PoK). Among the places where they were trained were Muridke, near Lahore, where the headquarters of the LeT are located, Manshera in the NWFP and Muzaffarabad in the PoK. Finally in Karachi.

Subjects in which they were Trained

Physical fitness, swimming, weapon handling, guerilla warfare, firing sophisticated assault weapons, use of hand-grenades and rocket-launchers, use of GPS sets and satellite phones, map reading, etc. They were given lectures on Islam and jihad.

Individual Weapons issued to them before They Left Karachi for Mumbai

One AK-47 rifle each with eight magazines, each having 30 rounds; one pistol each with two magazines, each having seven rounds; eight to 10 hand-grenades each; plus explosives with detonators and timers.

Communication Sets Issued at Karachi

Five GPS sets and five Nokia mobile handsets for the entire group of 10 terrorists. Of the five GPS sets, two were recovered from the group which had taken up position in the Taj Mahal hotel and one each from the groups in the Oberoi hotel and the Narriman House. The fifth set was recovered from MV Kuber, the Indian fishing trawler hijacked by them for sailing to Mumbai. One of the GPS sets recovered from the group in the Taj Mahal hotel contained the bearings of 50 places in Karachi. Another seized in Taj had the bearings of six places in Mumbai. The set recovered from *Kuber* had the bearings of the sea route from Karachi to Mumbai. The five Nokia handsets were manufactured in China. Three of them had been bought from a retailer called 12 Pakistan (Private) Ltd located in Clifton, Karachi. The other two had been bought from a retailer called United Mobiles, Pakistan.

Other Mobile Handsets used by the Terrorists

In addition to the mobile handsets, which they had brought from Karachi, the terrorists also used mobile handsets seized by them from Mrs Lisa Ringer and Mrs. Rita Agarwal in the Oberoi Hotel and Mrs Gabriage Harmbarg in the Narriman House.

Total Number of Calls Made by them and Received by them During the Attack

The mobiles used by the terrorists in the Narriman House recorded 181 calls lasting a total of 35172 seconds (roughly 10 hours), in the Oberoi 62 calls lasting 15705 seconds (roughly five hours) and in the Taj Mahal Hotel 41 calls lasting a total of 8834 seconds (roughly three hours).

My comments: The unusually large number of calls registered in the mobiles of the two terrorists in the Narriman House indicated that the command and control of the group was located at the Narriman House. Even though it has not been admitted by the Indian or Israeli authorities, it would appear that the Israeli authorities through intermediaries, including a Jewish person of Indian origin in New York, were trying to keep the terrorists in the Narriman House engaged in conversation. It is also learnt that the terrorists in Oberoi forced a Chinese woman from Singapore in the hotel to call the Singapore Foreign Office and seek its intervention. She was later killed by them. The terrorists were also contacted over phone by a private TV channel of New Delhi, which telecast the conversation.

Use of Internet Telephony

The telephone numbers were connected to an account created with CALLPHONEX, a VoIP service provider based in New Jersey, US. On October 20 and 21, 2008, an individual, who gave his name as Kharak Singh, intimated that he was a VoIP reseller based in India and was interested in opening an account with CALLPHONEX. For this purpose, two amounts were remitted. The first sum of US $250 was transferred on October 27, 2008 by an individual identifying himself as Mohammad Ishfaq through the Paracha International Exchange of Lahore, Pakistan. He gave a Peshawar address as his place of residence. The second amount of US $229 was transferred on November 25, 2008, by an individual who gave his name as Javed

Iqbal through Madina Trading of Brescia in Italy. While contacting CALLPHONEX, the man who gave his name as Kharak Singh gave his e-mail address as kharak_telco@yahoo.com. This address was accessed from at least 10 IP addresses — three of Gulberg, Pakistan, two of Chicago, two in the Moscow region of Russia, and one each in Lahore, Kuwait and Australia.

My comments: One of the IP addresses belonged to Col R Sadatullah, who was identified as belonging to a company run by the Signals Directorate of the Pakistan Army, which controls telephone and internet services in the PoK and the Northern Areas (Gilgit and Baltistan).

How the Terrorists Travelled by Sea from Karachi

Initially by a boat belonging to the LeT in Karachi called *Al Husaini*, which had a crew of seven. After entering the Indian territorial waters, they seized an Indian fishing trawler named *MV Kuber* in the Jakhau area. *Kuber* had a crew of five. Four of them were transferred to *Al Husaini* and taken towards Karachi by the seven-member crew of *Husaini*. Amarsingh Solanki, the navigator of *Kuber*, was retained in the trawler and forced to guide the trawler towards Mumbai. The terrorists transferred to *Kuber* from *Husaini* the consignment of arms, ammunition and explosives and diesel. They also transferred a rubberized dinghy with an outboard engine. At about 4 PM on November 26, 2008, *Kuber* reached a point about five nautical miles from the Mumbai coast. They reported over phone to their handling officer in Karachi. They were informed that the four members of the crew of the *Kuber* who had been taken in

Husaini had been killed. They took the cue and Kasab killed Solanki by cutting his throat. The terrorists inflated the dinghy with a foot-operated pump, transferred the arms, ammunition and explosives into it and with the help of the engine reached the Bhai Bhandarkar fishermen's colony area opposite Bhadwar Park, Cuffe Parade, at about 8-30 PM. Eight of the terrorists with their arms, ammunition and explosives plus telephone sets got down there. The other two earmarked for targeting the Oberoi/Trident Hotels proceeded to the hotel area in the dinghy. Of the eight terrorists who landed in the Cuff Parade area, the two earmarked for attacking the Narriman House walked to it. The two terrorists earmarked for firing in public places and the four earmarked for attacking the Taj Mahal Hotel went to their destinations by taxis.

Timing of the Attacks and the Fatalities

Railway terminus (From 9-50 PM to 10-15 PM. 25 minutes. 52 killed).

Cama Hospital compound and outside between 10-20 PM on November 26 and 12-15 AM on November 27. One hour and 55 minutes. Sixteen Killed — seven inside the compound and nine outside.

BPT Colony building. At 10-45 PM. Three killed.

Western Express Highway. At 10-50 PM. Two killed.

Opposite Cafe Ideal. 12-30 AM on November 27. One killed

Leopald cafe. Between 9-30 and 9-40 PM. Eleven killed.

Taj Mahal Hotel. Entered at 9-40 PM and stayed there till finally eliminated. 36 killed.

Oberoi/Trident hotel. Entered at 9-50 PM and stayed there till finally eliminated at 7 PM on November 28. 35 killed.

Narriman House. Entered at 9-45 PM on November 26 and stayed there till finally eliminated on November 28. Nine killed.

My comments: There is a discrepancy in totaling the fatalities. The total of the above comes to 167, but the police have totaled it as 166.

Total Fatalities

Indian civilians — 123

Foreign civilians — 25

Personnel of security forces — 18.

Nationalities of Foreigners Killed

Israelis — 6

Americans — 3

Germans — 3

Canadians — 2

Australians — 2

British, Belgian, Italian, French, Mauritian, Malaysian, Singaporean, Thai and Japanese — one each

Particulars of Security Forces Personnel Killed

Police — 12

National Security Guards — 2

Government Railway Police, Railway Protection Force, Home Guard and Special Reserve Police — one each

Estimated Damage to Property

Rs. 42 crores. This does not include the estimate of the damage suffered by the Taj Mahal Hotel.

My comment: One crore is 10 million. Rs. 48 equal to one US dollar.

ANNEXURE III

Pakistani Media Reports on the Press Conference of Rehman Malik, the Interior Minister, on February 12, 2009

By Mobarik A Virk (News of February 13, 2009)

ISLAMABAD: Pakistan on Thursday acknowledged for the first time that the Mumbai attacks were partly planned in Pakistan and that it has arrested six suspects, including the "main operator".

In its first detailed response to the dossier provided by India, Pakistan said criminal cases had been registered against nine suspects on charges of "abetting, conspiracy and facilitation" of a terrorist act. However, it said more evidence is required from India, including DNA samples of Ajmal Kasab, to establish his identity.

Addressing a press conference at the interior ministry, Interior Adviser Rehman Malik told the media FIR No: 01/009 had been lodged with the Special Investigation Group (SIG) in the Federal Investigation Agency (FIA) against nine suspects. The Pakistani investigators have identified Hammad Amin Sadiq as the alleged 'mastermind' of the whole conspiracy.

Malik said the cases against nine persons had been registered under the Anti-Terror Act (ATA) and the Cyber Crime Act and they would be tried under these two sets of laws. He said six of the nine accused named in the FIR have already been arrested and being interrogated, two have been identified but not arrested so far while investigations are still under way into the possible involvement of the ninth accused.

He identified those taken into custody as Zakiur Rehman Lakhvi, a Lashkar-e-Taiba (LT) commander who was arrested from Muzaffarabad soon after the Indian government alleged that the LT was behind the Mumbai attacks, Javed Iqbal, who was arrested from Barcelona, Spain, Hammad Amin Sadiq, believed to be the main operator belonging to southern Punjab, Zarar Shah, Mohammad Ashfaq and Abu Hamza. The name of the lone surviving terrorist now in the custody of India, Ajmal Kasab, is not included in the FIR.

He also said some of those arrested by the security agencies of Pakistan for possible involvement in the Mumbai attacks belong to the LT. Malik said Javed Iqbal, who was based in Barcelona, Spain, was the person who paid $200 for the 'Internet Domain' that was also used for communication and planning for the Mumbai attacks. "Having ascertained the involvement of Javed Iqbal, we somehow lured him into coming to Pakistan and he was arrested on his arrival," Malik said.

He also said the e-mail sent by 'Deccan Mujahideen' claiming responsibility for the Mumbai attacks was believed to be prepared and sent by Zarar Shah, who was responsible for communication link in the whole operation.

The adviser disclosed that the money to fund these attacks was transferred from Pakistan and was received in Italy. This money transaction was made through a Pakistani bank. He also said after thorough investigations by the Pakistani security and intelligence agencies it was learnt that these alleged terrorists operated from two bases — one inside Karachi and the other outside but not very far away from Karachi.

He also disclosed that the people involved in the Mumbai attacks used three boats for travelling to Mumbai, one named 'Al-Hussaini' and the other 'Al-Ghaus'. For communication, these culprits used 'Call Phonic' system and they also bought Indian cell phone SIMs for communication from inside India.

Malik said the findings have already been shared with the Indian government. The Indian High Commissioner in Islamabad was called to the foreign office and the report was handed over to him officially.

"We also have forwarded a set of 30 questions for which we would need answers as early as possible to support and further the investigation process on our side. We have asked the Indian government to provide us the DNA samples of the lone surviving terrorist, Ajmal Kasab, to ascertain his nationality, as we don't have any record of the individual with *Nadra* (National Database Registration Authority)."

"At the same time," he said, "we would like to have the statement given by Ajmal Kasab to the Indian investigators, how this group of terrorists managed to sneak past the Indian security and intelligence agencies guarding their coastal lines, and how these nine persons managed to travel in a small boat and reach the Indian coast".

He also pointed out that the satellite phone connection that was used for communication during the Mumbai attack was registered in the Middle East and not in Pakistan. He also said forensic reports of the arms and ammunition used in the attack have been sought from the Indian authorities.

The adviser on interior said to make a solid case against all these people who have been arrested or for whose arrest the Pakistani authorities are making all-out efforts, meaningful cooperation from India would be most important.

Agencies add: Malik said the breakthrough in the investigation had resulted from tracing the fishing vessel used by the militants, purchases of equipment like life jackets and the engine for the rubber dinghy that militants came ashore in Mumbai.

He said only nine of the 10 gunmen came ashore in the dinghy, and the fishing boat they had used to sail from Karachi had refueled on the coast of India's Gujarat state. The Pakistani official said one suspect was allegedly involved in the 2007 bomb attack on the Samjhauta Express in India that killed 68 people as the train headed for Lahore, and India has been requested for more information. NEWS 13-2-09

Islamabad hands over Mumbai probe report to New Delhi

By Sajjad Malik/Tahir Niaz (*Daily Times* of February 13, 2009)

ISLAMABAD: Pakistan has formally handed over the details of its investigation into the Mumbai terror attacks to India, the Foreign

Office said on Thursday as Adviser to the Prime Minister on Interior, Rehman Malik admitted that the attacks were 'partially planned' in Pakistan.

"The Indian High Commissioner was ... [on Thursday given] material pertaining to the Mumbai terror attacks probe by the Federal Investigation Agency (FIA), by the foreign secretary," said Foreign Office spokesman Abdul Basit.

Arrests: Meanwhile at a press conference, Rehman Malik announced 'breakthrough' arrests in the Mumbai probe, and admitted that the Mumbai attacks were partially planned in Pakistan. He said some of the suspects were linked to Lashkar-e-Tayyaba (LT). Rehman said a case was registered on Thursday under the Anti-Terrorism Act against eight suspects — including LT's Zakiur Rehman Lakhvi, Hammad Amin and Zarar Shah — on charges of "abetting, directing, conspiring and facilitating a terrorist act". Six of these suspects are in the custody of intelligence agencies, and all will be tried under Pakistani law.

"Some funds for the attacks were transferred from Spain and Italy," he said.

Karachi: Rehman said the suspects used three boats, all of which have been seized, to sail from Karachi to Mumbai between November 26 and 28, 2008.

More information: Rehman, however, said these findings were not final and Pakistan needed more information from India. He said the Indian authorities had been asked to answer 30 questions raised by the Pakistani investigators.

Other countries: The adviser said "the system of various other countries" was also used to plan the attacks. Rehman said two more men were being held, and identified them only as Khan and Riaz. Other leads pointed to Europe and the US, and Malik said Pakistan would ask the FBI for help. *DAILY TIMES* 13-2-09

Islamabad forex company involved

LAHORE: Interior Adviser Rehman Malik has claimed that a money exchange company in Islamabad was involved in transferring money to a suspect of the Mumbai attacks in Spain, said a private TV channel. The money was transferred through Paracha International Exchange's Euro 2005 branch in Islamabad to Javed Iqbal in Barcelona. The branch was later found sealed. Representatives of other branches have denied that such a transaction took place. But one of the two owners confirmed the transaction, and blamed his partner for it. *Daily Times* monitor *DAILY TIMES* 13-2-09.

INDEX